THE BEST IS NONE TOO GOOD

THE BEST IS NONE TOO GOOD

THE BEST

IS NONE TOO GOOD

By Ralph G. Martin

New York · 1948

Farrar, Straus and Company

ff

Designed by Stefan Salter
Manufactured in the United States of America
by H. Wolff, New York

To Al Kohn, Pete Paris, Greg Duncan, John Bushemi, and Bob Krell, the guys on the *Stars and Stripes* and *Yank* who didn't get to be veterans. And to Joey Black, who never even lived long enough to be a soldier.

This book isn't the final word. There are no statistics, no conclusions. I wondered what had happened to the men and women who had come home, and this is what I found. These are my impressions, these are the people I talked to. If there's a message in the book, you find it.

ACKNOWLEDGMENT

To the *New Republic*, where most of these articles originally appeared. Also to the *Stars and Stripes*, *Salute*, and *Yank*. The vignettes in this book were written originally for a six-part history of the European phase of the war which I did for the Paris edition of *Yank*.

For important help and criticism, special thanks to Ed Cunningham, Epida Epton, Graham Hovey, Murray Krim, Herbert H. Lyons, and E. A. Pastel.

For other help, thanks to: Harminny, The Turners, Larry and Guyo Tajiri, Loretta, Elias Herman, Bartley Dean, Artie, Esme and Carin, Harvey, Bob and Bea, Stan and Naomi Van Clair, Al, Dave, Bob, Pearlie and Sujy, Lee Gainen, Sadie, Jon and Marion Moon, and Herb and Bess, and Paul S. Green.

And without my wife Marge, this book would never have been written.

CONTENTS

THE BEST IS NONE TOO GOOD

An invasion ship is a lonely ship. Downstairs in an LST you sit and sweat and nobody says anything because there is nothing to say. You look around and you wonder who will be dead soon. Will it be that big tough-looking sergeant who is busy double-checking his M1; or the guy stretched out in his upper bunk who keeps praying aloud all the time; or the kid sitting next to you who wet his pants? Who will be dead soon?

Then the thought comes, swelling inside of you, a huge fist of fear socking at your guts, hammering and hammering. . . . "Maybe it's me. Maybe I'll be dead soon. . . ."

1

THEY MUST BE AWFULLY BITTER

THE man stuck his head into the classroom and said that he was sorry to interrupt again but the photographer wanted three more students for another picture in the Sloan Room. The teacher stared at him, then shrugged his shoulders and wearily motioned to several students near the door. Two of them picked up their crutches and slowly maneuvered themselves out of the room. The third got to his feet and walked out stiff-legged, the wood bumping against the floor, making a lot of noise.

"Why do they have to take all these pictures anyway?" a student whispered loudly. "Just to show that some more people without legs are going to school? Why don't they leave us alone?"

An older man in a heavy sweater, sitting next to him, just smirked and said in a low, bitter voice, "Jeezus, fella, they've got to take pictures. They want to show us looking happy so that the public will know how wonderful America is treating its disabled war heroes."

Some of the men in the near-by seats listened and snickered. When class was over, they all went outside for a smoke and some of the men were still talking about the pictures.

"Why do they always take all the pictures in that fancy, upholstered Sloan Room?" one of them asked. "Sometimes they ought to take a few in our dumpy little classroom. People ought to see how badly it needs a paint job and some good lighting."

Somebody then remembered how a photographer posed some amputees dancing at a hospital party. "They danced just long enough for the photographer to take his shot and then they hurried back on their crutches. But the photographer wasn't interested in that; he'd got his phony picture."

The ten minutes were up and the men tossed their cigarette butts into the slushy snow and filed back into class. Their teacher was waiting for them. He was a young, serious-faced naval officer who was teaching them veteran counseling. Their project that day, he said, was to have two students act out a practice interview. One student was to be the counselor and the other a maladjusted veteran.

Quickly the two men took their places on the platform in front of the class. A few of the students started ribbing the actors, but the ribbing stopped as soon as the student acting as the maladjusted veteran said, "I think I've been ill-advised. They sent me here to the American University to learn how to become a veterans counselor. Now I'm not sure I want to be one."

The room was hushed when the counselor asked him why he felt that way.

"Well, they've got all these men who come and tell us that we'll never make much money and how we'll have to work eighteen hours a day. Well, this is a tough course. We're learning a year's work in twelve weeks and we hardly get enough money allowance to live on. I got a wife, and at least when I graduate I want to make a decent living. And I don't want to work eighteen hours a day; I want to work only eight."

Spontaneously the whole classroom of thirty-five students started clapping. A few even thumped on the floor with their

[6]

crutches, and one student excitedly banged his wooden hand on the side of his chair. Their applause stopped only when the acting-counselor asked something else. He was asking why the veteran came to the American University in the first place.

"Nobody told me all these things before I got here," said the veteran. "But anyway I came because I'm disabled and I wanted to help other disabled veterans."

"So he came to the disabled American University," somebody said loudly in the rear of the room. The whole class again broke into a roar and the young teacher nervously tried to get them back into order again.

The students were still in a high flush of excitement when they went to their English class, a half-hour later. As soon as they sat down, though, their excitement seemed to fade quickly. There was no horseplay here. Dr. Don Wolfe was one of their favorite teachers; they had raised a stink when the school had tried to transfer him to another section.

Wolfe was telling them how continually amazed he was at the quality of their writing and that he was going to read from some of their themes.

He read in a sensitive voice, as if everything he read had happened to him.

"They belonged, and I was an outsider," he began to read from one theme. "How I ached for home. I walked the streets with that throbbing ache inside of me. How I hated anybody who had security. . . ."

There was no applause, no comment. The class was quiet.

The next excerpt was about a soldier who lost his right hand, telling in painful detail how he learned to tie his pajama strings and his shoelaces and how he shaved himself and how long it took him to learn to write left-handed so he could write a love letter himself, instead of dictating it to the Red Cross girl.

Following that, there was a series of combat stories, one of which ended with, "And nobody knows any other human being well enough to call him a coward."

Talking things over after class, Dr. Wolfe kept thumbing through the pile of themes. "I've got the whole war right here on my desk," he said. "They've scraped their souls and poured themselves out, things they probably never told anybody before."

Thumbing through the papers again, he picked out one entitled, "A Tough Battle: A New Life," by Irving Peltz. "This man lost an arm, a leg, and an eye at Anzio," he said.

At the bottom of page 5, Peltz wrote:

"I wanted to prove to myself and to everyone else that even though I was disabled, I could still do anything that anyone else could. My biggest obstacle was people. Yes, I said people! They practically broke down everything that I was trying to accomplish. I'd walk down the street and almost everybody would stop and stare. On the train, bus or trolley, it was always the same. In restaurants, they'd look up from their food. Damn them all! Can't they leave a wounded veteran alone? Haven't they got any sense? Don't they realize they make me feel like a freak? Why the hell can't they mind their own business?"

There was little noise or movement in the big room where the seven congressmen had been sitting for days, listening to a long line of witnesses tell what they knew about artificial limbs. It was the Labor Subcommittee on Aid to the Physically Handicapped. Peltz was on the witness stand.

"I got the limb," he was saying, "and it was terrific. It was like a two-ton truck. It kept irritating my stump, kept holding me back from getting well. As for the arm, it's of no use. The only reason I wear it is because it balances me in walk-

ing because I have a leg off, too. Nine out of ten amputees don't wear it at all. And the glass eye they gave me wasn't even a good fit. We've known about the need for better artificial limbs since World War I, but it seems to me that nobody has considered it important enough to do anything about it."

"Here's a couple more," said Dr. Wolfe. "They're both by a boy named John Regan. He lost his leg at Normandy." In the middle of one of them he wrote:

"My leg is torn to shreds from my knee to my hip. A bone sticks through this mess, pointing upward; I try to push it down but the pain is too great. I notice a colorless fluid flowing out; it reminds me of chicken broth. There is also an aroma coming from the wound, like that of a freshly roasted piece of beef. I try to stop the blood but without success. I become aware of the intense pain now. I am sweating and I am awfully thirsty. I start to rave out loud. . . . Oh God help us. . . . Our Father who art in Heaven. . . . Oh please, God, help. . . ."

Regan's second theme was shorter. It started:

"As I look around the room in this third-rate boarding house, there alongside the bureau is this *thing* . . . a leather cup, straps and buckles dropping from it. Below this cup, the flesh-colored part and calf and on its foot a brown sock and an ox-blood shoe. I've called this wooden leg a lot of things. . . . Oh, what the hell, a leg isn't everything. You've got to keep on living."

As soon as Representative Kelly introduced him, Regan showed the committee just how his leg worked with all the belts and straps. He told them how tough it was to sit down, that it was outmoded 100 per cent because it was the same

[9]

leg that amputees got twenty-five years ago. Then he told how it weighed thirteen pounds and he never wore it any more because it was too heavy. "It seems I wear it under the same strain as if I were running with two legs," he said.

"I realize I have a very bad amputation," he continued. "I realize that I am very lucky to be alive, but I feel that something should be done to make these legs lighter. All I ask for is a limb I can get around on comfortably. If the government and private companies can build a B-29, surely they can do this job. Remember there are sixteen thousand amputees coming out of this war."

When Representative Kelly thanked Regan and all the others for coming, a veteran named Robert Rogers jumped up and said, "We thank you for listening. Most people are scared to listen and say, 'Jesus Christ, let the Army look after you.' Of course they do nothing about it," he said. "We certainly thank you for listening."

"The American public ought to know about these things," said Wolfe, packing his papers into a folder. "Maybe I'll put them into a book some time."

Outside the small red buildings, the sidewalk was dangerously icy. Some of the students were slowly crossing the slushy street but most of them were still eating in the small luncheonette.

Several of the men were talking about a story in the newspapers telling how the government had indicted forty-five manufacturing firms of artificial limbs for agreeing on "identical and non-competitive prices," forcing amputees to pay several hundred dollars for a limb. The story also mentioned that the government had decided to spend a million dollars a year for prosthetic research.

A short, chunky man said it was about time, but that he

wouldn't believe it until it really happened. Another student said that's the way it was, that nobody ever got anything unless he yelled for it. He mentioned the grievance committee they had formed to get heat for their cold classrooms and the books that the Veterans Administration had paid for long ago. They had also bitched about the constant changing of teachers. Like the one teacher who had wandered in slightly bewildered. He told the class that he had just received this assignment the day before and what would they like him to teach them.

"I wish somebody would get up and yell about the allowance they give us and ask how we're supposed to live on it. If some of those fat congressmen would come and take a look at the rathole my wife and I live in and if they tried eating here in Washington on ninety cents a day—maybe then they'd get busy and do something," he said.

A tall man with one arm just laughed. "What the hell do you expect?" he asked. "V-J Day was a long time ago and people don't want to hear anything more about the war. As for cripples, nobody likes to hear about cripples. It bothers people."

There was a long pause and nobody seemed to know what to say after that, so they started getting up, paid their checks and walked out.

The cashier watched them leave and shook his head. "They don't kid around much any more," he said. "I've seen five classes so far and it's always been the same thing. When they first come here, they're all excited about the lucky break and they're always tripping each other with their wooden legs and then busting out laughing. I remember once they told me about this one guy who fell asleep at a party and the guys got all the girls to write their names and telephone numbers in lipstick on his wooden leg. When he woke up and saw the lipstick, he wiped it off; later he was sorry because he wanted a date."

He rearranged the chewing gum. "But that doesn't last long," he said. "They get nervous after a while and they don't laugh much. It takes three months sometimes before they get their first check, and some of them go around half-starved all the time."

A customer walked up, paid his check, picked up a toothpick and left. The cashier was still thinking. "I've been wondering," he said slowly. "They must be awful bitter about the world."

"One morning we looked up and there was a perfect blue sky and we knew that this was the morning of the attack," said Pfc. George Barrette, of Hillsgrove, Rhode Island.

"Next morning we moved into a patch of small pines, and they must have pin-pointed our CP because they threw in a six-hour barrage right on top of us. Me and this buddy of mine were in the same hole, with only a little brush on top, and I remember actually bawling. We were both praying to the Lord over and over again to please stop the barrage. We were both shaking and shivering and crying and praying, all at the same time. It was our first barrage. . . .

"When it stopped, both of us waited for a while, and then we crept out of the hole. I never saw anything like it. All the trees were torn down and the hill was just full of holes. They hit everything, even the battalion aid station. Every officer got hit except a TD officer.

"They sent me back to an aid station for a while and I guess they treated me for shock or something. Then they sent me back to my outfit. Everything was just as cold and slimy as it was before.

"And it was the same shells, the same goddam shells. Soon as I got there, the Jerries started laying them on again. They started laying them all over the road and I tried to dig in and then I started shaking and crying again. I guess I must have banged my head against a tree or something because I lost my senses. I couldn't hear anything. I don't remember exactly what happened but I was walking down the road and I remember seeing this soldier crawling out of a tank with both arms shot off. I remember helping him and then I don't remember any more. I guess I must have gone off my nut."

2

HUMAN ENGINEERING

The calliope sounded shrill in the stillness and the barker interrupted the "St. Louis Blues" to announce that the motorboat was getting ready for another ride down the Illinois River.

The people had come down to the park benches along the river front to cool off in the shade and watch the boats and listen to the old songs. They were mostly old people and kids. Old people sitting quietly, not saying much, and open-mouthed kids hugging the rail, watching the steamboat slipping in slowly.

An old-timer, a toothpick-chewing, big fat man with white hair, answered your question:

"The veterans? Heck, boy, they don't hang around here. They're workin'. Every veteran in this town that wants a job has got one."

Across the railroad tracks, down Main Street, past the post office, right next to a barber shop was a small store window with the sign, "Peoria Plan."

Peoria was different from other American cities because Peoria had a plan for its veterans; one so simple that no other city had tried it before. The crux of it is something they call "human engineering."

Talk to a veteran until he pours himself out, then decide

which tests to give him, add up the scores, make a graph, double check the tests with the talk—and you've got a "psychometric profile." Then you know whether to advise the Wac to get married or to open up a frozen-food store; whether that salesman should be an artist, or the unsuccessful artist should be a salesman.

That's mainly psychologist Barker D. Herr's job. And that's what makes the Peoria Plan unique—they have one of the most complete psychological-testing facilities in the country and their $125 examination is always absolutely free.

"But do you know the only tough thing about my job?" asked Herr, a man of thirty-five, with sharp eyes and a soft voice. "The fact that most people don't mind having their bodies examined, but when you start studying their minds and their personalities they get scared."

Eight tests or eighteen? The Minnesota Multi-Phasic Personality Test or the Kuder Preference Record or a Rorschach? Talk to him only for fifteen minutes or see him regularly every week? Names, faces, numbers, problems. Punch a hole next to the thing you would most want to do: (1) act as chairman of a social committee for a club dance; (2) decorate the hall; (3) send out announcements of the dance.

What do you see when you look at this ink blot?

Do you want to be alone all the time?

"But we never tell them what to do," explained Herr. "We show them what we find out, but the final decision is theirs. We simply try to help them to help themselves. And do you know who need the most help? The 'plus' people."

The plus people are those who have high IQ's but get poor grades in school because they are bored; the ones who are more mixed up than anybody else, more indecisive, have more emotional problems. Without proper guidance, they wind up as bank clerks when they should be bank presidents. They're the ones who get the most conference time, the most tests.

Not everybody says okay, you're the doctor. There are always those who say thank you very much, but I'll still do what I want to do. Almost invariably, though, they come back sooner or later to say, "You were right. I'm lousy in electrical engineering. What do I do now?"

Herr simply sends them, with their test results, into the next office to see McClellan.

V. D. McClellan is a former carpenter's mate second class, and before that he was a job specialist with the United States Employment Service.

"With me, there's no such thing as first come, first served," said brisk-talking, balding McClellan. He shuffled a big pile of file cards. "See these? They're all employers who have been begging me to send them veterans for different jobs. But I can't do it. I only send men to jobs they're fitted for."

When he does have a job he can fill—whether it's a truck driver or a baseball umpire or a radio-promotion man—he doesn't send a dozen applicants: he sends one. And the one generally sticks, generally pleases.

What's more, there's no filing and forgetting. There's the regular telephone checkup with both the veteran and his boss. Usually, everybody is happy about the whole thing, but sometimes the boss may say, "Well, the boy started out fine but we've been having trouble with him lately. He's always flying off the handle."

That's when McClellan sends him to Turow. Dr. Irving Turow, a small, mild-mannered psychiatrist who likes to listen to adolescents who matured in war, to men and women emotionally and mentally sick, to a new generation filled with fears:

"I tell you, doctor, I can't stand it any more. I know how

much he's been through overseas and I try to understand and sympathize, but there's a limit to how much I can take. Whenever we go anywhere, he always thinks I'm looking at another man. He's so insanely jealous, he's driving me crazy. . . ."

So many people with so many questions:

"Should I tell my wife all my sex experiences while I was overseas?"

"Somehow I always have the feeling that somebody is following me. . . ."

"I met her and we got married just before they shipped me. Now we're like strangers. Maybe it wasn't love, maybe we were just lonely. . . ."

"Every night I wake up screaming—every single night—got to help me, Doc. . . ."

Doc usually does. Often his psychotherapy is simply common sense. If it gets more complicated, he has separate conferences with the wife, parents, in-laws, and employer. To all of them he explains the tensions and the problems, the need for patience and encouragement.

Sometimes it goes deeper than common sense.

That jealous husband had a mother who was murdered by her lover; the machinist was so irritable because he had never learned to read and was embarrassed by it; and the frightened little man who was followed by shadows was a schizophrenic, serious enough to be hospitalized.

"But the general picture is bright," added Turow. "So many psychiatrists thought that our mental hospitals would be swamped with war casualties. I'm happy to say we were wrong."

Of the five thousand veterans treated here last year, there was a big group who wanted neither jobs nor psychotherapy. They wanted advice on GI insurance, disability payments, filing claims, going to college, or starting a business. Their man was a tall, graying veteran of both wars, Jacob Haberle. It was Haberle who made most of the early contacts with Peoria's organizations, businesses, prominent people. His file has three hundred names representing at least sixty different businesses and professions, all voluntarily pledging their time, money and advice to the plan.

If a vet wants to open a grocery store, there are business-men ready to tell him about the problems and the profits, lawyers to give him legal advice, bankers to talk about loans, real-estate men to help pick the location. With all of them it's a personal matter, not a rush act.

Besides Haberle, Turow, McClellan and Herr, there is director Jack Brennan. He has the job of smoothing the quirks and keeping out the politicians. When Illinois' Governor Green handed the Plan $50,000 for two years, there were no strings attached. The Community Chest supplied the rest, and former industrial consultant Brennan had a free hand and a lot of worries.

He's worried about long-range problems: which Peoria industries have expansion plans and what kind of job openings will there be six months and a year from now. He's worried about the growth of the plan. Oklahoma City and Jamaica, Long Island, have copied the plan, but he'd like to see it spread all over the country. It's come a long way from Dr. Harold Vonachen's original dream of it as a way to help disabled veterans only.

Some civilians have already started dribbling in. They come into the waiting room with a surprised look on their faces. They never knew there was such a place, a place where people cared about people, where a common, ordinary guy who worked in an office or a factory could come and pour out his frustrations. Like that listening clinic on the radio. Only

[19]

here they listened and did practical things. They found you jobs or doctors or schools. And you told your friends about it. And they couldn't believe it. Imagine a place like that absolutely free. What's the joker? What do they sell on the side?

The word has spread fast around Peoria. Every week the civilian customers increase; the veterans are fewer. Brennan sees the day coming soon when the business will be largely non-veteran.

"But do you know what my biggest worry is?" continued Brennan. "I'm worried about the eleven thousand Peoria vets who haven't yet come here. What's going to happen when all the veterans graduate from college and the 52-20 payments stop and the job market tightens up—what are we going to do if we have a serious depression then? Is there anybody in America today who is making any plans for that day?"

Well, Peoria has asked a question. Anybody know the answer?

When the soldiers hit a big town, some of them buy picture postcards to send home to the family. Picture postcards of big-bosomed babes holding bunches of grapes between their toothpaste smiles and wearing picturesque Alsatian clothes; or else pictures of beautiful mountain scenery and healthy, happy people, with an overripe yellow moon in the background.

They look at them without recognizing either the people or the places.

The beautiful babes aren't so beautiful any more. The healthy, happy people are hungry and thin. Those picturesque clothes have been lying in the bottom of the trunk for years. And this wasn't the season for grapes.

As for the scenery, that forest full of snow-covered Christmas trees was lousy with snipers; those thin winding streams running through the valley in soft curves only made their feet wetter; and the time that full moon shone on that row of dimpling hills in front of the fast-running Rhine, the Joes just looked at them and cursed quietly, thinking of the long climb, the mud, and the waiting mortars on the other side.

To frontline doughs, Europe wasn't picture postcards; it was scared, bitter people, dirty slush, and wild little kids eating out of garbage cans.

That's why so many GI's wanted to go home and stay home. They'd seen all they wanted to see of Europe, even though most of them had never really seen it at all.

3

LANA TURNER AND STALACTITES

If you're a veteran with a reconversion headache and you like the idea of being with Lana Turner in an atom-proof cave, write your Congressman for a job application. The job: guide at Carlsbad Caverns.

The whole atmosphere is a relaxing, family-style sort of thing, an ideal job for anybody with ulcers. The work isn't hard, not much boss pressure, and nobody punches any time clocks. Of course, the salary isn't much. If you want to get rich quick, you'd have a much better chance betting on horses—the right horses.

Ask Johnny Mosely. Johnny is twenty-eight, a handsome six-footer with a warm Texas drawl and this is the job he did before the war and the one he wants to keep on doing. He doesn't have to. His sister has been begging him to come to Dallas, where he could make a small fortune as a landscape architect. But, in the first place, Johnny doesn't like big cities. In the second place, he's one of those strange people who doesn't want to make a fortune.

And he likes to walk. That's another thing about this job, you have to like to walk. Five hours a day, five days a week. But you won't mind it if you're a scenery lover. Johnny is. He's seen the beautiful formations in the Temple of the Sun at least six hundred times and he still gets an emotional kick out of it.

There are all kinds of other attractions about the Caverns. Besides the fact that it's the best possible place to be if they ever start throwing around atomic bombs, it also has a convenient underground lunchroom. And the whole place is naturally air conditioned at a constant year-long temperature of fifty-six degrees. There are even some lovely clearwater pools for possible bathing on hot summer nights. It's really made to order for comfort, if you don't mind the three million bats.

Like every job, there are things to know. There are about three hundred basic questions concerning the caves, questions everybody asks, and you're supposed to know all the answers:

"How many miles of the caves are still unexplored? . . . Was the lunchroom here when they first discovered the caves? . . . Is the cute elevator girl married? . . . When do the bats come out to graze? . . . Is the water wet in these underground pools? . . . My little boy has to go— where can I take him? . . ."

And you have to have patience. When a smart-alecky geology student starts showing off what he knows about the hydrogen iron content of the water by asking technical questions, you're not supposed to kick him. But when someone (there is one in almost every large group) asks about the discovery of gold in the cave, guide protocol permits you to answer, "The only gold mine we have here is our lunchroom concession."

The thing is, you have to know who you can kid, and who you can't.

There was a big, heavy woman who was having trouble keeping up with the others on the long hike and Johnny sidled up to her, gave her a Gary Cooper smile, and said, "Say, you sound like a baby switch engine. . . ."

Since then, she's sent him ten perfumed letters.

It's also a good thing to know how to talk to 2500 people at one time. Some of the guides memorize their tour talk and sound like a canned phonograph record. Johnny is strictly on the informal side, improvising as he goes along. He's also mastered the technique of making people laugh so that they almost forget how tired they are and yet scaring them enough so that they don't try to take home a stalactite for a souvenir.

Then there are the women. If you're a happily married man, you better forget about this job. Many of the unmarried women tourists coming to Carlsbad are frustrated stenographers who have read too many love story magazines. When they see and talk to these handsome guides (you also have to be handsome) they get pitter-patter ideas in their hearts and often write long, passionate letters. Usually they don't even sign their names.

Johnny still has a shoebox full of letters, which he takes out and smiles at every once in a while. Here's one:

Dear Handsome:

Remember that slow-walking gal from New Orleans? Well, that's me. Sorry I didn't get to talk to you after the tour was over. . . . I just didn't know how friendly the women-folk were supposed to be with you guides. And I'm sure you get tired of being "sought" all the time.

P.S. Don't think I'm a bold "fem.", please.

To the question how friendly are women-folk supposed to get with the guides—the answer is: it depends. In prewar days, the summer guides, like Johnny, were mostly college kids. They had a standing bet on which one would date the prettiest tourist each day with a side bet on who would get the most fan mail.

It was a pleasant kind of living. One night you'd be riding in a limousine with a luscious South American babe and the next night you'd be discussing the Brooklyn Dodgers with a female from Flatbush. It had variety; it was nice.

Those were the crazy days when one of the guides went through a group of dudes (they call all tourists "dudes") shaking a flour sifter until somebody would ask what he was doing and he'd answer, loudly, "Oh, I'm sifting the crowd for a pretty blonde about five foot two." And he'd usually find her, too.

Those were the things Johnny would think and talk about on Bataan, just before he went on the Death March. There were two other ex-guides there and they'd get together and figure out the difference in time so they'd know where in the caves they would be if they were back. But of course, the times they were most lonesome for the caves were when the Jap bombers came over.

Maybe one of the things Johnny likes about his job now is that this kind of leisurely living makes a good transition from a Japanese prison camp to the land of milk and honey. Anyway, he's happy. And so if you too want to be a Carlsbad guide, you better apply now, the waiting list is getting longer.

By the way, the Lana Turner we were talking about in the beginning is actually the name of an interesting rock formation in the caverns. That's another thing about this job—you have to have imagination.

The hayloft was filled with the stink of dirty, sweating feet, but nobody seemed to notice. The men of the squad were stretched out in the straw, packed close together. Most of them were talking in low whispers; some were sleeping; a few were just lying still, smoking cigarettes, staring into the dark.

In a couple of hours, this first squad of the first platoon of Company A, 1st Battalion, 334th Regiment, 84th Division would be piling into an assault boat to cross the Roer River in the first wave.

The CO had ordered everybody to stay inside for security reasons. One of the boys had an ancient issue of some magazine and it had made the rounds, everybody reading every word in it, before it was put in the toilet paper supply.

"We were playing casino in the afternoon, because I'm the only one who has enough dough to play poker," said Pvt. Cletus Crawford, of Tama, Iowa, assistant bazookaman.

"I told the guys that if I kick off on this show, they're supposed to split my dough between them and play at least one hot game of poker in my memory."

The whole squad was wide awake now, everybody laughing.

One private said he was getting hungry and somebody told him to chew on his bedroom slippers and everybody got hysterical again. The private had asked for bedroom slippers when he was in England. They had just arrived that day.

"I don't know what to do with them," he said. Several soldiers suggested where he should stick them and that set off more laughs.

Sgt. Herbert Harding, acting squad leader, explained why everybody laughed so much:

"If we didn't laugh, we'd go nuts," he said.

4

DOCTOR'S DREAM IN HARLEM

THE VETERANS ADMINISTRATION WILL UTILIZE THE SERVICES
OF THE LAFARGUE CLINIC IN HARLEM, FOR PATIENTS OF ALL
RACES. IT WILL BE ONE OF THE FOUR PSYCHIATRIC CLINICS
RECOGNIZED IN THE CITY.

News Item

*It was the New York State Department of Social Welfare on
the telephone:*

"Sorry, Dr. Wertham, but we're refusing the request for a
license for your Lafargue Clinic."

"But why?"

"Because we've decided that there's just no need for a
psychiatric clinic in Harlem."

"Well, if there's no need for our clinic, can you please give
me the names and addresses of all the other places where I
can send my Negro patients?"

Long pause.

"Even if there is a need, we're still not satisfied with your
financial status."

"But we don't need any money. Everybody is contributing
his services absolutely free."

"Yes, but what about your rent?"

"That's free, too."

(Laughter.) "But for how long?"

"For eternity."

[29]

It all started fifteen years ago with a dream, a dream based on an idea, an idea that psychoanalysis and psychotherapy are not the private property of the rich but the common property of the people.

"And I don't want anybody to get an idea we're specializing in some interracial project, because we're not," said Dr. Frederic Wertham. "We're here in Harlem because this is where the need is the greatest. And we're not here to make a study of the Negro, because the Negroes' problem is just an exaggeration of what happens to all people anyway. Only here it's so much more naked and obvious. We're simply here to treat them like any other human beings."

He had a name for the treatment. He called it "social psychiatry." It meant that a psychiatrist had to understand a patient's economic and community life, as well as his sex life, before he could treat him properly.

Before the Lafargue Clinic was born in Harlem a short time ago, there was nothing and nobody for the mentally sick Negro. Except Bellevue. And overcrowded, understaffed Bellevue has an unenviable reputation in Harlem. Negroes have to be carried in there; few walk in. The few who do are told things like this:

"There's nothing wrong with you. You're a Negro. You think too much, that's all. . . ."

Or:

"Yes, you do need further treatment. We recommend that you see a private psychiatrist."

But who? Where? A white psychiatrist almost never accepts Negro clientele for fear of losing his rich white patients. Those who do, accept them only after regular working hours, and for much higher rates. As for Negro psychiatrists, in this country there are only eight who have been able to cut through the discriminatory red tape of medical schools.

But what about everybody else, the people who couldn't pay? The happy, normal fourteen-year-old kid who became suddenly obsessed with the fact of being a Negro and tried to kill two children so they wouldn't have to grow up into a world of prejudice; the little girl who became preoccupied with sexual problems because she lived with her mother, who was a prostitute; the woman who wanted to commit suicide because she was fired from too many jobs by bosses who saw her as a color instead of a human being.

What about them? Where did they go for help, for advice, for treatment?

They went nowhere. Theirs was a blank, blind wall. The suicide rate went up; juvenile delinquency in Harlem reached a high of 53 per cent of the city total. And a lot of people clucked their tongues and said what a terrible shame it was.

But nobody did a damn thing about it. Nobody seemed to care.

Except Dr. Wertham, who was still trying to peddle a dream of his. One supposedly liberal rich man listened to him, then smiled indulgently.

"My good Dr. Wertham, yours is a *magnificent* plan, but everybody knows that Negroes don't need any psychiatry. Negroes are just a happy-go-lucky people who are always able to laugh away their troubles. Besides, there are so many reasons why your dream isn't feasible. There are four hundred thousand Negroes in Harlem. A tiny clinic like yours won't even make a dent. And, my dear Dr. Wertham, do you honestly expect the Negroes to come to you, to trust you? One other thing. By placing your clinic in Harlem, aren't you actually practicing segregation?"

Dr. Wertham slammed the door when he left.

One night Wertham was discussing his dream with Richard

[31]

Wright and some Negro friends. Suddenly he said, "If we can't get the money to do it, let's do it without money."

They stared at him. "Well, why not?"

They all looked at each other and laughed. "That's right, why not?"

Assembling the staff was simple. There were several prominent psychiatrists, some of his former pupils, who had heard Dr. Wertham's dream a long time ago and were still excited about it. There was a young Negro psychiatrist just out of the Army who wanted to be part of the plan. Then four Negro social workers, a psychologist, and a secretary volunteered, and that was it. "When do we start?"

But that was the tough job: to find a rent-free place in Harlem for their clinic.

For months they went searching through the Harlem ghetto, where an average of 1,100 people were living on each acre, compared to 600 on the crowded lower East Side and only 266 an acre for the rest of the city.

They were still searching when Ralph Ellison suggested they talk to the Reverend Shelton Hale Bishop, of St. Philip's Episcopal Church. In Harlem, Bishop was the big push behind social-welfare projects, especially summer camps for kids.

Bishop was anxious to help.

"But, Dr. Wertham, all I can offer you are these two small, dirty rooms in the basement of our parish house."

"Father Bishop, that's wonderful. . . ."

The rooms were still dirty when the whole staff paid their first visit. Dirty and empty, except for a small red table and some benches.

But sitting on the benches, waiting, were the first two patients: a frightened young woman with big, pleading eyes and a man whose eyes were filled with emptiness.

And before they washed the windows or swept the floor,

they interviewed their patients. The woman had lost her job and spent all three hundred dollars of her savings for a psychiatrist who gave her ten shock treatments—which she shouldn't have had—and then dismissed her.

The man was a more serious case, so serious that Dr. Wertham dictated a letter to his secretary, who wrote it out in longhand because she had no typewriter. Father Bishop took the letter and the patient in a taxicab to Bellevue for immediate hospitalization.

The news spread fast, and every Tuesday and Friday evening people were waiting.

They were just people with troubles, all kinds of troubles. Real, practical troubles piled on top of psychotic ones. People who were frustrated because they lived in the rotten tenements of a dirty, filthy, ironbound ghetto; because they went to war to fight for a democracy they didn't have; because their kids had no place to play and were forming gangs; because they had poor jobs and worse pay; because their skin was black.

They were people pressed down into a feeling of miserable helplessness, pressed down so far that they were mentally and physically sick and tired of living.

So they stood there outside the door on Tuesday or Friday evening, patiently waiting for a psychiatrist to give them a thin slice of hope and meaning.

There were four psychiatrists, each in his own cubicle, separated from the rest of the room by screens. And afterward, if you had a quarter and wanted to pay, you dropped it in the box. Otherwise, everything was free. If you needed carfare to New Jersey, they'd lend it to you; if you didn't have enough money for medicine, they'd buy it for you. No red tape, no appointments necessary. You simply walked in off the street and nobody was interested in your skin color, race, religion, sex, or politics. You were just somebody who needed help.

"For me, one of the wonderful things about the clinic is that these people come here without fear on their faces, without suspicion," said one of the women psychiatrists. "They come here as if they've been waiting a long, long time for the place to open. And they have a pride about the place. They get a kick out of each new piece of furniture as if it belonged to them. One of my patients even said he was going to make a lamp for us at school. . . ."

"My dear Dr. Wertham, do you honestly expect the Negroes to come to you, to trust you. . . ."

Alongside one of the cubicles, the four Negro social workers were talking about their cases.

"There was one old woman who came here often," one of them said. "There was nothing wrong with her and she knew it, but she was just lonely. She just wanted somebody to talk to."

They have all kinds of jobs: check up on those who fail to keep return appointments, help find new jobs for those who need them, talk to parents about their maladjusted kids, figure out recreational possibilities where they don't exist.

"The big thing is to get the kids here," said the social worker in charge of children's case work. "We try to get them here while they're maladjusted and before they're delinquent.

"Because once they're delinquent, they don't stand a chance. The courts usually don't bother much with Negro kids; they send them directly to such places as the State Institution for Mental Defectives. They don't belong there at all: they come out of there bitter and mean and ready for crime. They belong in psychiatric clinics, where we can give them treatment, hope and direction."

He told about the Negro boy who had been taken to Bellevue for a psychiatric examination and the doctor said he had sexual fantasies because he sang a song that started out, "Don't you feel my leg because when you feel my leg, you're gonna feel my thigh. . . ."

"God Almighty," said the social worker, "everybody in Harlem knows that song. It's a popular recording. That psychiatrist just didn't know Harlem, that's all. Before he can diagnose that kid, he should know the cultural pattern of the community, what the kid lived through and how it affected him. That, again, is social psychiatry."

There were more people drifting into the room, going into the cubicles with the psychiatrists. Some stayed ten minutes, some a half-hour.

"I've been married for five months and my wife is frigid. . . ."

"People are after me," said the young girl with frightened eyes.

"I came back from the Pacific and found out my wife was sleeping with another man. I don't want to give her up but I can't forgive her. I got two kids. I'm going crazy. . . ."

"This is my mother. She was in an asylum and I took her out because I thought she was cured. But she's getting worse and I'm a nervous wreck now. I don't want to send her back to that asylum, but what can I do?"

A skinny, ragged kid in knickers walking in bashfully: "I cut my finger. Can you fix it?"

The door to the second room opened and Dr. Wertham came out laughing, waving a letter. "It's from the State Department of Social Welfare. They won't give us a license but they're already sending us patients."

He looked at his watch and his eyes twinkled. "This clinic was supposed to be closed an hour ago." Then he went back into his room with another patient.

"There's a great man," said his secretary after he closed the door. "I mean, besides being one of the greatest psychiatrists in the country. He's always doing things for people, especially the people that nobody else cares about."

She took out some letters. "Here's the response we're getting":

"Please accept my small donation of two dollars. I will try to send this every few weeks. Thanks for the privilege. . . ."

"Enough people talk and think sympathetically about conditions in Harlem, but too few of us do something about it. Please accept my small contribution. I wish I could give more."

The secretary leaned on the small red table, almost caressing it. "But the Doctor says that no matter how much money we get or how big we get or where we move to, we'll always keep this first table."

She thought of something and her eyes grew serious. "Better not use any names in the story. All these people have jobs during the day and you'd be surprised how many people hate us for what we're doing. They're afraid that other people will look at us and see that it can be done and maybe there'll be free mental-hygiene clinics sprouting up all over the city, all over the country."

She opened her arms, groping for words, "I only hope it does. . . . I hope the idea grows as big . . . as big as Dr. Wertham's heart."

It was Sunday in Colmar and all the people were dressed in their best clothes, walking down the Beethovenstrasse, going to church.

High in the dirty, misty sky, several Messerschmitts were slipping inside the flak, peeling off, diving down to bomb the city's outskirts. Shells were zooming so low over the city that you just kept wanting to fall flat on your face. Tanks, trucks and troops were rushing through the streets of the city in several directions. And on Beethovenstrasse, lying in a sticky pool of blood, there was a dead German sniper.

But except for a small circle of kids staring at the kraut, the civilians didn't seem to notice him, just as they didn't seem to notice the trucks or the tanks or the shells or the planes.

It wasn't that they were trying to separate themselves from the war by ignoring it. It was just that they had been seeing and hearing war for weeks now and it had become a part of them.

Now it was Sunday and Colmar was free and they were going to church.

5

CHICAGO WOULDN'T UNDERSTAND

NOBODY thought Pfc. Franklyn Paul Sandholm could live.

He had a big hole in his belly where a large chunk of a fifty-pound frag bomb had ripped through, cutting his bladder and small intestines, tearing through his rectum. Another fragment sheared away part of his arm.

That was ten minutes to ten, Sunday morning, December 19, 1943, in the outskirts of San Pietro, where Pfc. Sandholm and eight buddies were surveying advance positions for the guns of A Battery, 131st Field Artillery, 34th Division. Fifteen ME-109's had suddenly swooped out of the clouds and plastered the whole area, killing one out of the eight, wounding seven.

But today, after passing through one painful crisis after another on the operating table, absorbing bottles and bottles of slow-dripping blood plasma and spending fifty-five days in bed urinating through a tube—Sandholm was home again.

When you're stretched out on a hospital bed for a few months and you can't move, what do you daydream about?

"You can always get a job as rural mail carrier and Dad still wants us to live on the farm. Darling, you know you can still do a lot of things you like to do on the farm. You can still drive the tractor."

The tractor. That Chicago kid in the next bed would think he was crazy if he told him he'd been daydreaming about a tractor. Yet he had. Often. Anybody back home in Red Oak, Iowa, would understand the way he felt about it. The tractor was a symbol of his whole life. He had taken it apart and put it together so many times, he knew every screw in it. Driving it all day long in the fields, it was almost as if it were part of his own body. Chicago wouldn't understand that. Just as he could never understand how several hundred people could live in one big house for years and still not be neighborly.

There were 5,476 people in Red Oak and he knew every one of them. He could picture them right now sitting on their porches, swaying slowly back and forth on their rocking chairs. And he could see them smiling and waving at him while he walked down the street. Somebody once told him you could measure a man's life by his real friends. How many real friends did Chicago have?

But not all his friends were coming back. That one day when Company M of the 168th got swallowed up at Faid Pass. God Almighty, Company M *was* Red Oak. All the baseball teams and the drugstore cowboys and the whole high school graduating class. He still had that newspaper clipping that said if New York City had lost a proportionate amount of men in a single action, it would have totaled twenty thousand. But even then the shock wouldn't be so bad in New York; it would be just a list of names. In Red Oak, every name meant a certain house on a certain street. It was such a small town. . . .

He walked slowly out of the farmhouse.

Before he knew it, he had his overalls on and had gone into the barn and said hello to May and Nellie. He had raised them since they were colts, and they recognized his voice and whinnied at him. Then Rover smelled him and jumped at him and licked him all over. Rover was sixteen years old. That's pretty old for a dog. He thought he'd be dead.

And then he went out in the field and saw the tractor. . . .

The sniper's finger presses the trigger and the bullet passes through the helmet, scalp, skull, small blood vessels, membrane, into the soft sponginess of the brain substance in the occipital lobe of the cerebral hemisphere.

Then you're either paralyzed or you're blind or you can't smell anything or your memory is gone or you can't talk or you're only bleeding.

If a medic picks you up quick enough, there's a surgeon who can pick out the bullet, tie up the blood vessels, cover up the hole in your head with a tantalum metal plate. Then, slowly, you learn things all over again, whether it's talking, walking, or smelling.

But if the bullet ripped through your medulla region in the back of your head (about twice the size of your thumb) or if it tore through a big blood vessel in the brain—then you're dead, buddy.

It all depends how your head was curved when the bullet hit.

6

HOOD RIVER ODYSSEY

IF YOU had never heard of it before, you would have thought that Hood River was just another town, a quiet place sitting in a frame of mountains at the end of the winding loveliness of the Columbia River gorge. But if you remembered things, you walked down the streets searching for signs that weren't there. Then, finally, you asked somebody where the court-house was.

Because, even though you had never been here before, you remembered the courthouse best of all. You had heard about it on one of those slushy December days in 1944 on the Seventh Army front in France. It was a small story in the *Stars and Stripes* telling how the Hood River American Legion Post had wiped off the names of sixteen Nisei soldiers from their honor roll on the side of their courthouse building.

You remembered all this so vividly because you had asked some 26th Division soldiers what they thought about it. They were all alive that day because a Nisei regiment, the 442nd, had punched through to save their starving, cut-off "lost bat-talion." Most of what they had to say about Hood River you couldn't print.

So now you walked quickly toward the courthouse and looked up at the long columns. Even in the dimness of twi-light, you could see the freshly repainted names of the Nisei.

Why did they fight in this war, anyway? Well, some went because they would have gone anywhere to get out of the barbed-wire concentration camps into which the Army had slapped them. The rest, because they wanted to prove to the world that they were as good American citizens as anybody. Only a bitter few said no, thanks, why the hell should we?

Not Fred Hachiya. They gave him the Silver Star when they buried him in Leyte.

And not Sagie Nishioka, who just got his forty-second blood transfusion. Nishioka wrote a letter, which the Reverend W. Sherman Burgoyne read in his Hood River pulpit, saying that he had already forgiven the misguided people who had broken into his home and smashed or "borrowed" his fine furniture. His one wish now was that some day he would be able to come back and work in his pear orchard.

While Burgoyne read the letter aloud, the stores in Hood River all had signs in their windows reading, "NO JAP TRADE." Kent Shoemaker, local Legion bigwig, was running a full-page weekly ad in the town paper saying once a Jap always a Jap and don't believe all that baloney that they didn't commit any sabotage here and would you want your daughter to marry a Jap?

Shoemaker also featured a poem which read:

> *Hood River, Golden Valley of the Hills,*
> *Who is to possess its acres and rills,*
> *A horde of aliens from across the sea*
> *Or shall it be a Paradise for you and me?*

Signing the ad were dozens of Hood Riverites who wanted the paradise for themselves. Most of them were farmers who had rented land from the Nisei and wanted to keep it. This now-rich land was once unwanted stumpland, given to Japanese workers in lieu of wages before the First World War.

". . . . That's another thing I don't like about those damn Japs. They work too hard. Unfair competition. . . ."

"As we have said time and again," protested Kent Shoemaker, when they rubbed off the Nisei names, "there is no economic issue involved in our action. This is our America and we love it. Can *any* good American blame us for wanting to preserve this beautiful valley for *our* posterity?"

From Pearl Harbor, Marine Sergeant David White wrote home: "Why did you do it? We're ashamed to say we're from Oregon now, much less Hood River."

Somebody else wrote: "If you rub off those sixteen Nisei names, take mine off too."

The payoff came when Kent Shoemaker's own soldier son, Ed, wrote a letter to the editor saying how much he disagreed with his Dad, how proud he was of the Nisei friends with whom he had grown up and who had proved their citizenship ten times over.

But when the War Relocation Authority mailed pamphlets to the people of Hood River asking them to practice democracy when the Japanese American evacuees returned, one Shoemaker stooge returned the pamphlet with this letter:

Gentlemen:
This paper is too stiff for the purpose I would like to use it.

The tension reached a crucial tightness in January, 1945, when the first three Nisei returned. Ray Sato, Min Asai and Sat Noji walked down Main Street and saw people look through them as if they were ghosts. In front of the poolroom, a few of the regulars stared at them and spat. And when Ray saw an old friend and rushed over with his hand outstretched, the old friend gave him a glassy look and walked right by. And the kids jeered, "Japs . . . Japs . . . Japs . . ."

Everybody waited for an explosion. The town grapevine

rumored lynchings, burnings, beatings; the three Nisei slept together at Ray's place and waited for the worst.

It never came. The town whispered that some F.B.I. men had come down and warned Shoemaker & Co. that they would be held responsible for any violence.

Then a few of the signs came down. A gas station operator named Kramer announced that he had decided there was no difference between a Nisei Japanese and a Nisei German and he was a Nisei German.

Another sign came down when a former marine captain who had had Nisei in his outfit came back from the Pacific and pointed to the sign in his father's store window. "What the hell is this, Dad?"

But Nisei who walked downtown still said they felt they had signs on their backs, "Shoot here." When Mrs. Avon Sutton waved hello to Edna Abe on Main Street, Edna rushed over crying, "Mrs. Sutton, you're the only friend in town who said hello to me." When Kikue Tabara tried to sell her asparagus crop, the produce man said nothing doing unless she got a white person to sell it. He didn't want any of his friends to know he was buying Jap goods, he said. Kikue's husband was overseas at that time.

Then when Bob Kageyana went into the barber shop for a haircut, the barber fidgeted for ten minutes, neither waiting on him nor kicking him out. When Bob finally asked him about it, the barber muttered, "But I've got a son in the Army. . . ."

"Well, what do you think this is, a Boy Scout uniform?"

Then, suddenly, strange things happened. The owner of one of the movie theatres stopped a Nisei on the street to say how welcome Japanese Americans would be in his place. Also, several storekeepers, hats in hand, visited their old Japanese friends to tell them how much they missed them at their stores.

They weren't kidding.

Ever since the four hundred Japanese Americans had come out of their concentration camps back to the valley, these town merchants had watched the evacuees spending all their money in near-by towns. They needed all kinds of equipment to replace everything that had been broken and stolen and lost while they were away. They weren't buying in Hood River because the signs were still up.

So, one day, the signs came down, all of them.

The merchants decided that they were no longer afraid of Kent Shoemaker's boycott pressure and they didn't want to lose out on all this money.

Mrs. Max Moore, a big, friendly woman, one of the few who never had the sign in her window, had an added explanation for the change.

"It's mainly because most people in Hood River are really good people. As for the noisy few who started all the trouble, their convictions weren't as deep as ours. Theirs was mostly a bluff and now I really think the bluff is over."

Something else that spiked the bluff was the fact that people like Ray Yasui had made sure that every one of eighty-five eligible Nisei had registered to vote. The word got around. And in Hood River eighty-five votes are a lot of votes. So when the politicians were considering candidates for county judge and somebody suggested Kent Shoemaker, the politicians all screamed at once, "Are you crazy?"

The final touch to embarrass the race-haters was the stagey demonstrations of friendship every time a Caucasian vet saw one of his Nisei friends downtown. That prompted a lot of town organizations, like the Booster Club and Veterans of

Foreign Wars, to send invitations to various Nisei to come back again into community life.

Somehow, though, the Nisei aren't rushing back. It takes time for their hurt to heal, and they've been hurt so much. All those signs, blank looks, boycotts, threats, hate. It will take time for Ray Yasui to rub away the look on his five-year-old daughter's face when she came back from the grocery store this spring, whimpering, "Daddy, they don't like us in there, do they?"

Because the pushed-down race hate in Hood River still exists:

The farmer who said, "I don't like those lousy Japs but I'm not doing anything about it because I'm mixed up in a lot of farm deals with them."

Oldtimers, like Post Commander Jess Eddington, who still run the American Legion post here, mutter that they would never have repainted the Nisei names if it weren't for a direct order from the National Commander.

"No sir, we ain't ashamed of what we did, but we can't fight the whole country."

Shortly after November 29, 1944, when the names were wiped off, the Reverend Burgoyne, the Methodist minister, attacked the action as undemocratic and unchristian. Burgoyne and a small handful continued to fight until their stand became known throughout America. Letters poured in from all over and people asked what they could do to help.

To each of them, Burgoyne sent this answer:

"The battle for American decency happened to take place here this year. We fought it and won. Next year it may be in your part of America and I'm counting on you to stand true."

What do you do up front when it's quiet?

If there's a sun, you take off your shoes and socks and wiggle your toes in the warmth of it. If it rains or snows, you try to get under cover somewhere. The chow gets better and you eat hot meals a little more often maybe. You put in for a three-day pass to anywhere. You sleep as much as you can.

You sweat out your turn for a hot shower and you stand in it as long as they'll let you. You want to stay in it for hours and hours and you rub yourself with soap again and again, trying to get the stink out of your body and mud out of your mind and the war out of your soul, for a few minutes anyway.

Then you climb back into your dirty, smelly clothes and go back to your muddy foxhole up where the war is.

7

THE BEST IS NONE TOO GOOD

No QUESTION about it, said the vice-president of the University of Missouri. Veterans here are a healthy influence on education. They work harder, make their teachers work harder and raise standards all over the place.

It was too bad that the country's colleges weren't really prepared for the veterans. But when the University bought 165 government trailers, it was a gamble. Who could be sure that veterans would even live in trailers? And nobody ever thought that the housing situation in town would get so terrible. Nobody even imagined. . . .

Now it's too late to get any more trailers, and there are almost nine hundred married veterans on the waiting list. The state just gave them six million dollars to build permanent brick apartments, but materials are hard to find. Temporary barracks are being put up, but the vets will still be a little crowded—144 to a big barrack. It is too bad we couldn't see what was coming and plan for it. Because there's no question about it, the best is none too good for our veterans. . . .

HOUSING

In Trailer No. 335, twenty-six feet long and eight feet wide, live Jon and Marion Moon and their baby daughter, Sandy. Complaints?

"Let's walk around and you can see for yourself."

Big, shiny, private trailers parked so close to small, warped ones that their radio programs seem to merge. A man mows a pitifully small lawn, only three steps each way. Flowers and vines and curtains try to color some of the drabness. The bottom covering of one trailer is so torn that you can see water dripping down from the icebox into a smelly, stagnant puddle crowded with flies. Mothers yell for their kids. The stink of the garbage shed, overflowing cans, more flies. A dirty boy carries a big pail of water to his trailer.

In the center of the camp stands a white wooden house badly in need of a paint job. Here are the toilets, showers, washing machines. The washing machines are all broken, the women's showers scummy dirty, and there are quick-crawling roaches everywhere in the toilet, under a sign saying, "Remember, this is your HOME. Keep it clean."

"They've just tarred our trailer roof for the eighth time to try to stop it from leaking," said Marion Moon. "Sometimes we wake up in the morning and there's an inch of water on the floor. The main reason we're so worried is that Sandy is susceptible to pneumonia; she's already had it three times. But then one of the maintenance men told me that all these government trailer roofs are rotten. You can ask Mr. Ashlock."

Thin, sad-looking Norman Ashlock sitting in his corner office in Jesse Hall, with maps of the three trailer camps, a pin for every trailer. Behind each pin are people like the Robert Sconce family. The stove broke down in the winter when it was so cold they hardly had enough covers for the baby. Their trailer roof sagged so in the center that Bob bumped his head every time he stood up. And twelve other specific complaints.

When they saw Mr. Ashlock he referred them to Mr. Johnson of the Veterans Administration, who referred them to Mr. Brady, vice-president of the University, who referred them back to Mr. Ashlock. And when Ashlock finally came around to investigate, he walked inside the trailer and stood up and bumped his head.

"Mr. Ashlock, what do you do about these leaky roofs?"

"We keep tarring them."

"But it doesn't seem to be working."

"You got me," he said, shrugging his shoulders and smiling resignedly. "I don't know what we can do. They're all old trailers, you know. One thing about trailers, there's not much room to dodge leaks, is there?"

And what about the dripping iceboxes, scummy showers, broken washing machines, roaches?

"That's what we hire maintenance men and janitors for. That's their job. Besides, you seem to forget that those veterans are lucky to be in those trailers in the first place. A lot of vets don't have any place at all to live."

SOCIAL LIFE

The beautiful campus here, with the ivy-covered columns and the greenery, is quiet. Lots of people, but not much noise. No rah-rah college spirit. The faces are older, more serious.

At Gabler's, the juke boxes are still screaming, but the faces are those of the outnumbered teen-age freshmen, their razz-ma-tazz only slightly subdued. Most veterans take their dates elsewhere, someplace where they can get beer and quiet. They go big for plays and concerts, too. This year, for the first time, there are going to be repeat performances of every concert.

For married veterans, who have to pinch pennies, social life is made up of an occasional bridge game, a rare movie, long walks in the moonlight.

"If we only had some privacy," said one dark-haired woman.

"I like my neighbors, but we all wish we weren't so close together, so cramped. I've almost forgotten what it feels like to walk into my own bathroom, to have it all for myself. As soon as my husband graduates, we're going back to our apartment and I'm going to parade around naked all day, just to feel the sheer luxury of privacy."

For the wives of veterans, there's only the monotony of conversation, waiting for their husbands to come home. And when the men get through with classes they've got homework and studying to do.

"When I went to college before the war, I went to have a good time," said ex-marine Randall Mitchell. "Now I want to learn something."

They're not kids now; they've been in a war.

FINANCES

Do you know what ninety dollars a month buys today, Mr. Government?

"Sure, my wife and I live on ninety a month, sometimes," said Norman Holman. "But that's when we don't do anything. I mean things like shows and ice-cream parlors. That also means no clothes. I'm still wearing my army stuff. What's more, my brother brings us meat and vegetables from his farm every once in a while. But even then. . . ."

The University takes care of maintenance, subtracts costs from rent, hands the rest over to the Federal Public Housing Authority. Rent until recently was $15 a month. The University announced that it just covered costs. Then the FPHA raised rents at M.U. ($5 more if you had other income, $3 if you hadn't).

But why? Why should they pay $15 a month for a better trailer with running water down in Arkansas and $25 for one in Minnesota? Why shouldn't all veterans, who were given the same $65 or $90 a month, be charged the same rent for the same trailers? And why should the government make profit on this money? It didn't seem fair; it isn't.

The veteran who can't get a trailer, the married veteran who was No. 700 on the waiting list, has to try to find an apartment or a room in a cellar that sometimes costs as high as $65. Some have bought trailers with their savings, hoping to sell them after graduation. For a single vet, it's a question of finding a bed anywhere. If it costs too much, he doesn't go to college.

A tall, thin man said he had spent $1,100 of his own money since he had come to college. He considered himself lucky, he said, because he had the money to spend. He had been a lieutenant. "But what about the poor Joe who was an enlisted man, who wasn't able to save as much as I was?" he wondered.

"My question is," he said, "Is a college education worth all this?"

EDUCATION

The hell with snap courses.

That's their attitude now. They say: "I'm interested in what I can get out of this course, what I can really learn. And I want a prof who teaches, not preaches. I've had enough indoctrination. I'm not the schoolboy I used to be. I'm not just going to copy down every word he says. If I disagree, I'm going to question; if I don't understand, I'm going to find out why."

It's a big problem, said David March, political science teacher, also a veteran. Teachers have to change their whole approach. They are no longer teaching merely seventeen-year-olds; mostly they teach mature men.

To teach these mature men, Missouri is now hiring a new crop of young ex-high-school teachers, teachers who still emphasize the conjunctive adverb instead of the thought, who ask test questions on dates instead of history.

"I'm getting out of here. What's the point of going to college when I get some dumb young punk of a teacher who isn't any older than I am and doesn't know much more? Everything he's taught me, I could have got out of a textbook. He practically reads the thing. And we've got 250 guys in our class."

His friend was listening quietly, then added: "It's true that what a guy learns in college depends largely on himself; but in college they're supposed to make it easier, not tougher."

Arthur Ferrer shook his head. No matter what anybody said, he was grateful and happy to be here. College had always been a dream of his. If it weren't for the Army, he'd never be here. He had never even graduated from high school, had had to pass an entrance exam to get in here. What he couldn't get out of teachers, he'd get out of books. Maybe the Army gave him a rheumatic heart, but it gave him a chance for a college education. No, sir, he just didn't have anything to bitch about.

"These veterans are all so important," said one professor, "because they're going to run the world, and if they don't run it well, we're just not going to have a world.

"At a time when our colleges should offer the best teachers and the best education, they're the most inadequate. We still haven't made the decision whether we should fully educate five hundred or half-educate a thousand. I just hope we make that decision before it's too late."

You cross the river in small rubber boats late at night, feeling wonderfully thankful that you're in a reserve battalion coming up late and nobody is going to get killed crossing this part of the river now, because the other battalions have secured the high ground on the other side and the Jerries don't have any more direct observation on the river. But then you stop feeling thankful because it's raining like hell and every part of you is wet; you're going to have to sleep in the mud and you're going to have to dig your hole into it and you know that you are going to have to dig with your hands because the mud will stick to the shovel. And you know you're going to have a choice soon: dig a hole two feet deep and sweat out the incoming freight more than usual, or dig it deeper so that the water seeps in and you're practically swimming but you get better protection from shrapnel.

You have a choice.

8

CASTLES IN THE AIR

The room was packed with people who spilled out into the hall, down the stairs, and formed a line that stretched almost the length of the block to the corner of Harrison Avenue. Inside this Bronx office of the American Veterans Committee, interviewers were calling out numbers.

Number 103 sat down heavily and the first question came quick and cutting: "Are you disabled?"

Stanley Billauer, once a private with the 3rd Battalion, 357th Regiment, 90th Division, started to smile, as if he had thought of something funny, and then he said, "Yes, I'm disabled."

He and his wife were living with his folks but they wanted a place of their own, he said. They wanted three rooms, and if they couldn't get that, then they'd take two, and if they couldn't get two, they'd take anything. Only it would have to be on the ground floor, he said, "because this is a new leg I've got and I'm not really used to it yet."

In the next few minutes the interviewer explained the whole setup. As soon as the Waves moved out of these 11 buildings, the landlord would make 600 of the 750 apartments available to veterans selected by the AVC. The selection was based on a priority system, with the Purple Hearts coming first, and then those who were overseas longest. Doctors also received special consideration. But the apartments couldn't be ready until some time in January or February. The interviewer's final advice was, "Don't stop looking."

After Billauer had left, the interviewer seemed puzzled. "I don't get it," he said. "I've had six amputees so far this morning and you'd think that at least some of them would start bitching, but none of them have. I tried to get a reaction out of the last guy, and do you know what he said? He said, 'Why should I be mad? At least I have a roof over my head and a cot to sleep on.' And I thought they'd all be so bitter."

Next to sit down was a young plump girl with frightened eyes. "Everything's happening next month all at once," she said nervously. "I'm gonna have a baby and my husband's getting discharged and so is my brother, and where we all gonna live?"

She was living with her mother and her brother's wife and children in a tiny three-room apartment, she said. For months now she had read all the newspapers, gone to all the agencies, and walked up and down the streets but she still hadn't found anything. While she was talking, she kept staring at the interviewer's face and then, suddenly, she broke down. "Please don't discourage me," she said. "I've been discouraged so much already, I came here all the way from Brooklyn."

When she left, the interviewer wiped his face. "Jeezus, what the hell can I do?" he said. "My wife and I can't find anything, either. We've been living with her folks for two months and that's two months too much. And I don't even rate on this setup here because I wasn't overseas long enough and I never got wounded."

The numbers kept running quickly into each other, and every story was something special:

"I am looking for an apartment for my son. He was an infantryman with the 45th Division in Germany. Right now

I'm sleeping on the couch so he can sleep with his wife in my bed. But I've got a wife, too. . . ."

"My wife and I got two wonderful kids and we're living in a dirty hole full of rats and cockroaches crawling all over everything, because we couldn't find anyplace else. How can you raise kids in a place like that?"

"No, I don't have any husband. He was killed in the Philippines. I've been living with my girl friend, but now her husband's getting out of the Navy. I don't know where to go. . . ."

"You mean to say you don't have any furnished apartments available? Well, you're certainly not very efficient around here, are you?"

"My son Sammy doesn't want to come home. He lost both legs at Anzio and he says he won't come home until we move to some other neighborhood. You see, he was born and raised in this neighborhood and everybody knows him and he just doesn't want any pity. . . ."

"Look, we just got married a couple months ago and my wife has to sleep at the Y.W.C.A. and me at the Y.M.C.A. What kind of marriage is that, anyway?"

"Listen, mister, I don't want any sympathy, I just want a place to live."

The room was full of noise but the noise stopped completely the minute a tall AVC member got on a chair with a white piece of paper in his hand. "I want your attention, please," he said. "We just got a letter from a landlord who wants to rent a three-room flat. There's no hot water but there is a private toilet. The rent is seventeen dollars a month. Is anybody interested?"

Several people came quickly to the desk to get the address, including a thin little man who said apologetically to nobody in particular, "This is just in case we can't get anything else."

The man who made the announcement went back to his

crowded table to sort out the rest of a big batch of mail. His name was Irving Katz and he was just discharged. He was a lawyer, he said, and was helping out here because he knew what it meant for six people to live in two rooms. Then he shoved over some of the letters.

One was from a man who said he couldn't understand why the city didn't buy up some of those huge, deserted estates on Long Island and build a lot of homes for veterans. Another was from Halloran Hospital and certified that Pfc. Martin Slitsky, ASN 3252744, was paralyzed from the waist down and couldn't be released unless he had an apartment on the ground floor or in a building with an elevator. Still another letter, on expensive blue stationery, was from a man who said that his heart was touched by the veterans' plight and he would be glad to sell one of his houses to some needy veteran for $4,500.

Then there was an eight-page letter that said: "All of a sudden out of the Deep Blue Sky, everybody is looking for apartments. I think that everybody that is not born in these five boroughs should be sent back where they belong. All veterans that are born in New York and Brooklyn, Bronx, Staten Island, Long Island should stay here and the ones that are from out of town should go back to Washington, Chicago, and South California."

Bunched in the back of the room, waiting for their numbers to be called, several new civilians were saying something similar. They were saying that the farmers who went to work in the shipyards during the war ought to go back to their farms.

"But it isn't as if there aren't any empty apartments in this town," said an air-corps lieutenant who still wore his uniform. "I was talking to a real estate friend of mine and he told me there's supposed to be a 25 per cent turnover of apartments in this town every year, war or no war," he said, beginning to get angry. "It's just that a lot of sonofabitch superintendents won't rent you an apartment unless you slip them a couple hundred bucks first. I know a guy who shelled out five hundred for his place. And the landlords just don't seem to pay any attention to what's going on."

"Hell they don't," said a big, heavy guy who might have been a master sergeant or a major. "A lot of those landlords got private rackets all their own. They throw a few pieces of broken-down furniture into an apartment and then say they'll only rent it to you if you buy the furniture. My buddy paid seven hundred bucks like that, then threw the junk out as soon as he moved in. Somebody ought to crack down on those bastards."

There was a minute's silence because some more numbers were being called out, then an ex-corporal with a lot of ribbons and six battle stars broke out bitterly, "I'll bet this place is a racket, too. If I slipped those interviewers some dough, I'll bet I'd get an apartment in a hurry."

Somebody on the fringe of the crowd, who had been listening, interrupted, "You're all wet there, bud. These guys are good Joes." He pointed to a busy interviewer with a black mustache and glasses. "That one's a doctor. He takes time off from his practice to help out." Then he pointed to a short, thin man. "And that guy was in the same outfit with me in France. He should be looking for a job instead of helping here."

The corporal shrugged his shoulders. "Well, maybe I'm wrong then," he said grudgingly. "Maybe this one is on the level. I've bumped into so many phonies, though, that I'm suspicious of everything."

From there the talk shifted to solutions. Nobody seemed to be very happy about the idea of living in prefabricated houses in Flushing, even if it was temporary. It was too much like the old army barracks all over again, they said. Oh, they'd live there all right, they'd live anywhere, but it just wasn't the kind of thing they used to dream about in those waterfilled foxholes. The same went for the plan of converting substandard flats into something livable by installing toilets and hot water. One quiet, little man said that the way he understood it, the reason for the big delay in building was that construction materials were expensive now and all the builders were waiting until costs went down.

"It's the same old story," said the corporal with the battle stars again. "You fight a goddam war and you finally come home and everybody slaps your back and tells you what a wonderful job you did and all that crap, but when it comes to really doing something, then nobody's home. Nobody seems to know from nothing. All you get is words."

There was a pause after that, everybody silently agreeing. Then a young ex-sailor told the story of a cousin of his whose husband was overseas and she was so desperate to find a place to stay that she answered an ad for a governess. It was a nice room and a nice kid. But then the kid's father decided that he wanted just as much attention as the kid.

"Before she finally got out of the house, he almost raped her," said the sailor.

The big, heavy guy smothered a laugh. "If I have to get raped to get an apartment, it's okay by me."

The laughter that followed was broken up by the interviewers bawling out more numbers. This time several of the group got up in a hurry. Soon, the only ones left were the quiet, little man and the young sailor. The little man nodded his head toward an end table where a Negro was being interviewed.

"That's another reason why it's difficult to get apartments," he said in a low voice. "A lot of landlords don't advertise their apartments because they're afraid that colored people will try to rent them, and I think there's some kind of law now that you can't refuse an apartment to a man just because he's colored."

The Negro being interviewed at the table was a big husky young man who said he had just come back from three years in the Pacific with the aviation engineers. His name was Robert Cottrel and this was his first stop on an apartment hunt, he said. His wife was going to New York University and he was looking for a job here. He had a theory, he said, that many Negroes created their own walls of segregation.

"Of course," he added slowly, "I don't want to live where I'm not wanted."

Hours later, when only a few people were left, the interviewers relaxed over some cigarettes.

The only woman there told of her last applicant, a young girl who recently had had triplets, whom her husband never got to see because he was killed in Germany. Well, the girl now lived with some relatives in a crowded apartment on the fourth floor and she had to make two trips up and down to carry all the babies. She was thin and weak to begin with, and just couldn't take it any more. She wanted a ground-floor place.

"Well, what do you want me to do, cry on your shoulder?" said the lawyer impatiently. "They're all tough cases. She and two thousand others, and all we got is six hundred apartments. I can't understand why the state and the city didn't plan for this a long time ago. They knew it was coming."

"There was one sailor who had a funny idea," said the man who had a pants business in Passaic. "He said that instead of scrapping all the LST's, the government ought to line them up along the docks and convert them into houses."

"What's so funny about it?" said the lawyer. "It's better

than puptents in Central Park. Somebody better do something soon, that's all."

Everybody said goodnight and the only ones left in the office were the policeman from the 44th precinct, a man fixing the telephone, and Katz. Somebody knocked on the door and the cop looked inquiringly at Katz, who finally nodded resignedly and the cop unlocked the door. It was a poorly dressed little woman with a firm face who promptly opened up with, "Please, me no speak English so good. Me got four sons in Army and my man was hurt in last war and we always try so hard to keep whole family together and now my sons come back and we have no room for them. Please, mister, do you know place with more rooms for all of us?"

Later, when the policeman said goodnight, all he could think of to say was, "It all seems like such a damn shame, don't it?"

A mortar squad is only a temporary family. The faces are always changing in a mortar squad. The same goes for an infantry squad or an MG squad; the faces are always changing.

If any one face hangs around very long, it gets older fast. War makes a man out of a kid who never shaved, or it breaks him.

"I came in at Sicily brand-new," said Sgt. Willis Spencer of Company B, 180th Regiment, 45th Division. "I didn't know my tail from third base. I was only nineteen. I was only a private then, too. Then pretty soon another guy gets knocked off and another guy and another guy and pretty soon I'm the oldest guy in the squad, so they make me a squad leader.

"Then Salerno and some of my new guys get knocked off and I keep getting more and more new guys and they keep getting knocked off. At Anzio it was the same old story. I guess I must have had about five different squads.

"I don't know how I happened to hang around all this time. Maybe I'm just lucky."

9

THE GRAVY TRAIN

In a well decorated Hollywood living room, several friends were having their after-dinner smoke.

"Now take those veterans in the 52-20 clubs. I tell you, the government is making bums out of our boys. Why should those boys work? They're living off the fat of the land. . . ."

They were waiting out in the rain, the mob of them, waiting for the doors to open. Then they filed in quickly, filling up the long lines without too much noise, as if they had been doing it for a long time now. They simply stood in line, shuffling slowly toward the clerks' windows. There was no laughter and not much talk. If you looked at their faces, you could feel some of the shame in their silence.

In this huge unemployment insurance office in Los Angeles, only a few of the veterans knew the answers. The rest talked in question marks.

The short, almost bald man didn't want to give his name. He still had some pride left, he said. "Not much, but some."

He used to be a rug salesman in Detroit. War made him a radar specialist and the Navy discharged him with a back disability. "No more rug handling," warned the doctor, "do something else." Anybody want a middle-aged man with

[71]

fifteen years' sales experience? When Detroit said no, he came to Los Angeles.

"Everybody here tells me they've got their own returning veterans to take care of," he said, rubbing his head. "Do you know the only job offer I've got so far? Night janitor at thirty-four a week."

He looked up. "You know what? I may even take it. What can you do when you've got three kids?" He shook his head. "But you'd think that with fifteen years' sales experience. . . ."

It was his turn next at the window and the woman asked him automatically if he had been available for work during the past seven days. He just nodded. When she handed him his check, he stuck it into his pocket and, without looking at anybody, headed for the door.

It was like a game. You walked down a line slowly and suddenly you stopped and looked at a face and asked questions. This one wasn't ashamed to give his name. "The hell with it," he said. "Who gives a damn?"

He was a big heavy guy, this Leo Zale—formerly employed as a rifleman with Company I, 105th Regiment, 27th Division. Before that, he had been a crane operator in a shipyard, a jack hammerman in a gold mine. "Even tried to get a job as a painter's helper but they tell me I haven't got enough experience. Well, where in the hell am I supposed to get experience?"

He talked loudly, his voice full of bitterness, about the sign in the harbor, "WELCOME HOME, BOYS—JOB WELL DONE"; and about how he slept on the beach for the first five days after his discharge because no one had a room for him. "You can write that in your little notebook."

His voice got softer. "And my wife left me. I've got a four-year-old kid I've never even seen."

What about his old army buddies?

"Most of them died on Okinawa." He half smiled, "I was supposed to be lucky. . . ."

Walking up and down the lines, you only saw the tiredness and the bitterness. Inside the offices, all was sweetness and light. The small, round man, who didn't want to be quoted, you understand, said that everything was fine and dandy. Things were really picking up, yes siree. Fewer than nine thousand veterans were coming here every week for their checks now, while once there had been sixteen thousand. Matter of fact, the colored boys made up half the load now. You know what they say about those colored boys—last ones hired, first ones fired. Just can't find jobs for them. No siree. Same with the Mexicans and the Filipino and Japanese boys. Yes, sir, if it weren't for them, our office would have a lot better record.

You couldn't tell this to Harold Vaughn. He sold his bootblack stand on Hollywood and Vine to enlist in the Army. It has been nine months since he had a job. His wife's having a baby. Last ones hired; first ones fired.

And the broad-shouldered Mexican American, an engineer-gunner on a B-17 who spent most of the war in a PW camp in Nuremberg. He was an experienced bookkeeper, he said. Had all kinds of references. Almost a year without a job. "How do you think a grown man like me feels to have his wife support him?"

There was the very young Nisei vet who was so shy he blushed when you spoke to him. He had been out of work for a long time but this was his first check. His face flushed deeper when he said slowly, "And I don't think I'll come here again."

On one line there were three women: one, a tall girl, Joy Windsor Kennedy, was mad because nobody would hire women truck drivers; the second was bubbling redheaded Evelyn Wheeler who was convinced she'd make a fortune once she graduated from a millinery course; the third was a pretty

[73]

petite Wac, still in uniform, who didn't smile when she said she wanted to be an actress.

The bums were there, too. The small, rotten handful. You could almost close your eyes and listen to the few loud voices and pick them out. Like that song lyric, "They were jerks before they went into the Army, and now—they're still jerks." They were the ones here who were bitching so loudly about the length of the lines; the red tape, the weather, and how they could get all kinds of wonderful jobs for all kinds of money but they didn't feel like it right now. They were the ones who went back home and told their friends about the government gravy train, how every 52-20 club member was having a paid vacation. A few bad eggs giving a stink to the whole setup.

One loud mouth was telling his uninterested neighbors on the line that he was opening a big store in Hollywood next week. A little man with an old face asked him why the hell he was standing here on line if he had so much dough. The big, handsome, blond guy slapped the little guy on the back, "Why not, bud? It's free, isn't it?"

Behind the big desk the man said that almost eighty thousand veterans had filed initial claims at this office alone, but that there were fewer than twenty-five "exhaustions" a week —that is, twenty-five vets who had received all fifty-two payments.

In other words, the job picture was a shifting thing. The faces changed. A vet would take a job, quit, come back for his unemployment checks, take another job, quit. They'd do that until they found something they liked to do, something with security and a living wage and a future. Then they'd take root, he said. The big trouble was that most jobs paid so little, he added. Lunches and carfare brought thirty-dollar salaries down to the same thing 52-20 gave for free, so you could hardly blame some men for quitting.

But not everybody here was groping for hope. Bill White still knew how to laugh. A tall man with a thin mustache and without a line on his face, he had just arrived from Minnesota in a homemade trailer and wasn't worried: "Who ever heard of a good interior decorator starving to death?"

Jerry Rice also knew what he wanted. But when Rice laughed it was wistful. Thirty wasn't old, was it? Okay, so maybe he wasn't as snappy as these kids who tried out for chorus boy jobs. But then he didn't want to be a chorus boy. He had gone through that routine. Pasadena Playhouse, Shakespearean Festival, summer stock companies, even a few bit parts in movies; an up-and-comer going places.

Well?

He shrugged his shoulders. "It's remarkable how many different ways people can say no. The interviewer here keeps telling me there are no jobs for actors, that I should try something else. But I told him, what's the use of my life if I can't do the one thing I want?"

Martin Yoho, of Fort Scott, Kansas, and Corregidor, had the same problem. Only he had no choice. He had kept up his boyhood dream of being a mechanic, but three years and four months in a prison camp did something to his eyes. His last job was packing crates.

"They fired me because they said I wasn't interested enough in my work." He hesitated. "I guess they were right."

Near the door, Harold Berger was waiting for the heavy rain to stop. He had quit a good-paying job in an upstate New York post office to come here, he said. He was going to write scripts for his old army buddy who was master of ceremonies at a big Hollywood night club. They were going to tie up as a team and travel all over the country, maybe even Europe.

He talked quickly, brightly. Then he looked at the check in his hands and his face sagged. His eyes followed the short line to a booth in the alley. "CASH YOUR CHECKS HERE— ONLY A DIME."

The words came out more slowly. "I hope you didn't mind the monologue," he said. "I talk that way every once in a while to try to convince myself. My friend was in the Army too long, so he lost his contacts. Me, I'm broke." He flicked his check. "If it wasn't for this. . . ."

"We were dug in at a cemetery at the edge of St. Lô. Two platoons of Company C of the 1st Battalion of the 134th Regiment of the 35th. And we stayed there three nights and everybody was kidding about this was sure a helluva place to dig in, a helluva thing for our morale. But nobody laughed very loud because it wasn't very funny. We had just taken Hill 122 outside of town and out of two hundred in a company there were forty left. That's not very many. And we had to stay in this cemetery because our artillery was still shelling the town. So we stayed there; but the krauts knew where we were and shelled the hell out of the place. All these dead being unburied again and all these caskets and then the terrible stink of fresh dead horses and cows. We lost some of our boys too. There was one guy who was split right in half. I remember specifically. No, we didn't bury any of our own dead. The Quartermaster does that. I think they take them back to an American cemetery, don't they?"

10

BEST JOB IN THE WORLD

A BEARDLESS young man wearing a yellow sweater and a pork-
pie hat was staring at a huge poster inside the Army Recruiting
information room. Splashed all over it were pictures of soldiers
having fun in different parts of the world. Then, in big type,
the message: "Enlist Now. . . . Vacation, Travel, Security,
Education, Career, Good Pay, Liberal Retirement Benefits.
. . . The Best Job in the World."

He kept looking at all this lingeringly, and then turned to
examine the men waiting in line at the information desk. For
a few minutes, he just stood there, hesitating. Then he walked
quickly out of the room.

Sitting on the sidelines, watching everything wistfully, Felix
Bezubek told how much he wanted to re-enlist. "If I was single, I'd jump at it," he said. "I'd be right there on that line
with those guys. Honest to God I would," he said, slapping his
knee.

"And why not?" he went on. "You don't have to worry any
more about somebody else's cousin taking your job, you know
that your wife is going to get a pay check every month rain or
shine, and, no matter what you say, it's a good, healthy life."

He smiled weakly. "But my wife doesn't see it that way. She
says she waited three years for me to get out of the Army and

now she wants me to stay out. You can't really blame her. She was pretty lonely. But then I guess all women are like that."

He explained that he had just brought his nephew down to enlist. "Now if I was as young as he is. . . ."

At the information desk, the three long lines merged into one and soon disappeared. Sergeants Joseph Smith and George McCourt both took a five-minute break.

Things were picking up, said McCourt. They had been getting more than four hundred a day for the past week. Mostly veterans and young guys.

"They want to know all kinds of things," he continued. "One guy wants to know if he can go back to England right away because there's a girl there he wants to marry in a hurry. Some of the kids want to know if they'll be shipped straight to college or whether they can drill in the daytime and go home at night. I had one guy who wanted to enlist in the worst way. He had one big problem, though; he was still AWOL from the Marines. We had a jockey the other day, too. He said he was enlisting just to get away from horses for a while."

The phone rang and Smith grabbed it. First he listened, then he asked, "How old are you?" He listened again and then smiled tiredly over the phone, "Well, I'm sorry, bud, but you'll have to get your parents' permission first."

"You get real funny ones over the phone sometimes," said Smith. "Like the one who called up to find out where he could enlist in the Navy. Then the one who asked if it made any difference how many kids he had. When I said no, he got all excited and said he was rushing right over. It turned out he had eight kids."

"That's nothing," McCourt continued. "We had one guy who had ten kids. Counting allowances and everything, he'll get about ninety a week from the Army, which is a helluva lot more than he got as a gas-station attendant. Besides all that, he's stationed in a recruiting office in Flatbush and he goes home every night. That, brother, is a sweet setup."

A small Negro girl wearing glasses, her hair braided in long pigtails, walked timidly up to the desk and asked McCourt something in a low voice. McCourt answered, and her eyes got big and frightened and then, very slowly, she turned and walked away.

"She wanted to join the Wacs," McCourt told us. "But they're not taking any more."

"We get a lot of women calling us up," Smith added. "Mothers call up to find out if their Willie was here. Then we have wives hunting for their husbands."

"I had one like that yesterday," McCourt went on. "She was really crying, too. Said that she didn't have anything to eat and no place to stay. I didn't know what the hell to say, so I told her to call the Red Cross."

Smith pointed to a woman sitting in the corner wiping her eyes. "She's been there all day. We get lots of them."

Two more lines had formed and McCourt and Smith went back to work. There was a short, sharply dressed man with a big cigar in his mouth who leaned over and asked, confidentially, "Say, chief, what's the latest inducement you got for officers?" The next one wanted to know if he could learn how to be a photographer in the Army. The third, who looked slightly bewildered, simply wanted to know, "Can you please tell me where in hell Pier A is?"

One kid silently handed over his application blank. McCourt scanned it in a hurry and asked, "Where's your father's signature?" The kid blushed, then blurted out, "My pop's in jail."

All those with completed applications moved into the back room, where they sat down on one of the long wooden benches.

A few were reading newspapers or talking in low voices, but most of them just sat there, glumly.

"Why am I re-enlisting? What do you think?" exploded Larry Gilchrist, who was still wearing his uniform and a Pacific Theatre ribbon. "Because I can't eat promises and because my wife can't and my kids can't, that's why. I've tried this civilian life for three months now and you can have it. When you've got a family, you need a job that pays enough for you all to live on. And I couldn't find it, that's all."

Several seats away a young recruit was asking questions of a veteran who was wearing civilian trousers and an officer's blouse. He had been an MP lieutenant in Germany with the 83rd Division. Once upon a time before that he had been manager of a restaurant in a food chain. When he went back there, he saw a line of job applicants two blocks long.

"Besides, I wouldn't want to work for that food chain any more anyway," he finished. "They put too much chicory in their coffee." He tried to smile.

His young listener with the thin face was John O'Neill. A returning veteran had taken his job, he said. That was okay with him, but there was nowhere else to go; it was the same all over. That left the young guys just sticking out in the middle of nowhere with no future. He couldn't afford to go to college and he had to support his mother, so he figured the Army was the best bet. "If a guy isn't a first-class jerk, he can learn a lot of things in the Army. And I'm not exactly an old man yet. I'm seventeen."

A big, heavy Negro came into the room, looked around for a seat and finally sat down next to two Puerto Ricans. He was thirty-nine-year-old William Blackwell, he said, and if he couldn't be a mechanic in civilian life, then he'd be one in the Army. "Because I'd feel kinda wasted, starting all over again as a porter for twenty-five bucks a week." He had tried hard to get a mechanic's job. "But you know, we're the first ones fired, the last ones hired," he told them, almost as if he were reciting it.

The two Puerto Ricans listened without saying anything. One of them was Rafael Figueroa and he spoke so softly you could hardly hear him. He had come to New York from a tiny place called Cayey and his cousin had found him a job making cushions in a factory. Then he went into the Army for four years and had been discharged a few months ago.

"But I don't get used to civilian life," he said. "I go back to cushion factory and all people different, everything different. So I come back to Army now. Besides, I no like to make cushions any more."

His friend, who had bright white teeth and a lively smile, put in that he was joining up mainly because he wanted to be shipped back to Puerto Rico, where his family was. "I have lots girl friends there too," he said, winking. "Maybe some of them married, but maybe some still around waiting, huh?" He started laughing.

A sergeant called out a long list of men for fingerprinting and almost everybody in the room lined up. Across the hall, another group, already partially processed, was waiting for the next step.

James Pegram said he used to be with the 870th AAA Battalion on Okinawa. "Hell, I remember when I was sweating out discharge. All I wanted was to get away from the brass hats and the red tape and the regimentation and the chicken and be a civilian again."

He paused. "So now I'm a civilian. So what. I used to think the discharge button would mean something, but it don't mean a damn thing. Everybody's got one. There's lots of places where you can buy a button for a buck and nobody asks any questions. I couldn't find a job, couldn't find a place to live

—what's the good of that button? So now I'm thinking that maybe the Army wasn't so bad after all."

Several benches away, a bald-headed warrant officer was very happy about the whole thing. He had twenty-seven years, nine months and four days of army service and now he was going back to get the rest of it. If he was thirty years younger, he would do the same thing all over again, he said. His job in the Army? He was an assistant band leader. As soon as he was retired he planned to start a small music school. He had already bought a little home with his savings. "Yes, sir," he said, smiling, "you do your job in the Army and you get along very nicely."

Some corporal came through the room and announced that there would be a thirty-minute break for lunch and the mess hall was just down the street. The rooms quickly emptied.

Only a few still stayed where they were. There was a tall, husky young man wearing a big-checked wool shirt who said he was Whitman Snyder of East Islip, Long Island, and he was just seventeen. He was joining the Army to see the world. Paris, Berlin, Tokyo, Africa, all those places. "Look how old I am, and yet I've never been outside of New York City."

No, his mother didn't like the idea too much, but you know how mothers are, he said. Anyway, she finally gave in. Yeah, maybe he was just a little bit scared, but don't worry about him, he'd be okay.

One of the men getting ready to leave wore a merchant-marine uniform. He was ruddy-faced, blond, heavy-set, with deep circles under his eyes. He was Tom Curtis, from Boston.

"Do you really want to know why I'm enlisting?" he began bitterly. "Do you want the real God's honest truth? Well, I'm enlisting because I want a place to sleep. I'm tired of sleeping on the benches at Penn Station. I've been sleeping there for three weeks, and I'm tired of it, do you understand?"

He was standing and he sat down again. "I'm tired of the dirty looks they gave me at the Pepsi-Cola canteen just because I'm in the merchant marine. I'm tired of not having enough money to eat a full meal and I'm just goddam tired of everything, that's all."

He didn't want to ask his folks for money because he felt he was old enough to take care of himself now. Sometimes he worked part-time as a bus boy for three dollars a day. Then he'd try to get a bed at the Seaman's Club, but they were always full. For a while, he slept in the cocktail lounge of the Hotel Pennsylvania until an assistant manager found him and kicked him out.

The worst thing about sleeping on the Penn Station bench was that you had to sleep with your shoes on, he said. Then at four in the morning, the Penn cops would come around and wake you up to ask if you were waiting for a train. And you couldn't lie to them, because then they asked to see your ticket. The only thing to do was to move out until they left and then come back and sleep until six-thirty, when the next shift came around. "They all know me now," he added.

"And that's my why's and wherefore's. I'm joining the Army because I forgot what it's like to sleep in a bed and because I want to get three squares a day, every day." He was eighteen years old.

Through the door was the last big room, where a score of typists were interviewing the soldiers, pounding out the final records.

"Sure, it's interesting," said Mildred Bayarsky. "Every guy is something different. I must say that some of them are fresh and impolite, but most of them are just bewildered. Some of them won't talk unless you ask them questions, and others will just talk your arm off all day long if you let them."

She told how some of them poured out their most personal

problems, telling all about their love life, and how their wives ran away or their sweethearts married another guy.

"I'll tell you," she went on, "some of them are so nervous and their hands shake so much that they can't sign their own names. I have to promise that I won't look at them while they sign it. And some of them are so young. . . ."

Partitioned off from the big typing room was a smaller room with an American flag standing in the corner. The lieutenant was bent over, rapidly signing his name to a big batch of applications which he then handed to a sergeant. You could hear the sergeant calling out the names over the steady noise of the typewriters. Then they filed in. Some veterans in mixed uniforms, some scared-looking youngsters, two veterans in full uniform with all their ribbons, their shoes smartly polished.

The lieutenant asked for final questions, but there were none, and then in a high-pitched voice he started, "Raise your right hand and repeat after me. . . ."

It had been such a long day. All day and all night riding in trucks with the same old K rations to eat, sleeping in your clothes as usual, a single blanket maybe to cut off the night wind. Just some sniper fire and a few isolated machine guns to wipe out. Nothing much.

Two buddies stretched out together off the road:

"You know, Willie, I'm scared. I'm so goddam scared. . . ."

"Are you nuts? The way we're going now, the whole thing will blow over in a couple of weeks. Then you can go back to your wife and make babies and tell all your kids what a wonderful hero you were."

"That's what I'm scared about, Willie. It's almost over and I'm almost home and I'm scared that maybe just a lucky shot will get me. And I don't want to die now, Willie, not when it's almost over. I don't want to die now. Do you know what I mean?"

"I know what you mean. . . ."

11

THEY'VE FORGOTTEN US

THE small roped-off section of the cold cellar was filled with people waiting to hand their slips to the busy woman behind the desk. This was the welfare section of the United Electrical Workers Union in Bloomfield, New Jersey, and these people were striking workers wanting food. There was no conversation, no smiles. They all just stood there, quietly, waiting their turn.

A mother came in with her small daughter. She was a long thin woman with tired eyes and a shawl over her head, and her daughter had blond curly hair. As soon as they walked in, the daughter broke away and pointed to cans of food on the shelves, bursting out with, "Look at all the food, Mama . . . Mama, look. . . ." Everybody in the room stared at the kid. Still, nobody said anything, nobody smiled.

Standing behind the desk, a short, stocky man was directing three men who were struggling with baskets full of food. "We've got some more stuff coming in from St. Aloysius soon. Don't forget to check it before you bring it in," he warned. They nodded and left.

The man at the desk was James Hull of the union's food-procurement committee and he was worried. "It keeps getting tougher and tougher to get food," he observed. "The house-to-house campaign has slowed down and we've soaked the town merchants pretty hard and they're not doing much business right now. Everybody's been good to us."

His voice took a higher pitch and he waved his hands. "But what are we gonna do? We're feeding nine hundred of the seven thousand strikers right now and every day we're getting more and more. I stay awake nights trying to dream up new schemes to get more food. I keep thinking of all these people who need it so bad."

He told about the speeches he's been making at churches and union meetings, how one union shelled out $380 by passing the hat and how lots of other donations were coming in through the mail.

"It's when things are blackest that something wonderful pops up out of nowhere," he went on. "Like this invitation we just got to send eighty-nine speakers to eighty-nine different Negro churches in New York this Sunday."

So far, he himself wasn't getting any of the food because he still had some money saved up. Not much, but some. "This food is for those who don't have anything," he said.

Some more men came in carrying baskets and Hull excused himself. "Go over to one of the locals," he suggested, "but come back later."

In the narrow, crowded store where Local 412 had its headquarters, people were busy typing, telephoning, talking in small groups. In the back, a middle-aged man was patiently showing a pretty volunteer just how to work the mimeograph machine. Near the window, Albert James Arman was apologizing for not taking me to his home:

"I'm ashamed. Honest, I'm so ashamed that I never invite anybody to my home. Because it really isn't a home. It's just a two-room, dumpy, slummy rat-trap. And if the plumbing stinks up the house or if a light switch breaks down and if you ask the landlord to fix it, he just says, 'If you don't like it—

move.' It's bad enough we live there; we never have any guests."

By "we" Arman meant his mother, who has been bedridden for the past fifteen years, and his younger sister. He had had to quit school at fourteen to help support the family.

"Things were pretty rough then, that depression and everything," he continued, "but now they're even worse. And this is supposed to be prosperity. Hell, I'm thirty-eight and I can't even make enough money to get married."

He stopped talking to stare at the girl operating the mimeograph machine. "Get married," he blurted out, "that's a laugh. That's almost hysterical, it's so funny." He kept looking at the girl and then gradually quieted down. "I had a girl once. Wonderful woman. Search all over the world for a million years and I wouldn't find anything better for me. When I was in the Navy, we wrote each other all the time. All kinds of plans we had. We weren't sloppy romantic, you understand, but we had hopes and dreams.

"Well, we broke it off. I know it's a dirty deal. She waited so long, and all that. But what the hell was I to do? Take her into the fifteen-dollar flop we got and support her and my mother and sister all on thirty-four dollars a week? That wouldn't be marriage, that would be hell."

He was rubbing his hands, looking at them. "I don't know what kind of future I've got. Maybe I don't have any," he went on. "Anyway, I'm going to high school at night. I want my diploma. Can you imagine a guy my age still going to high school?" Quickly, he looked at his watch and said he had to go. He was due on the picket line soon.

Standing near-by, dark, heavy-set Anthony Tennelli admitted that he hadn't registered for union welfare yet. "It's my lousy pride, I guess," he said. "But I've never taken anything from anybody in my life and I just don't like to start.

Besides, we still have a couple more twenty-five-dollar bonds. After that?" He shrugged his shoulders.

He and his wife lived together with his wife's diabetic mother and her sixteen-year-old sister, who was still going to school. Just before the strike started, his wife had a baby.

"Funny thing about that kid," he added. "Ever since we got married, that's all my wife and I could talk about—how we wanted a kid worse than anything in the world. Doctor and hospital bills used up most of my mustering-out pay, but I didn't give a damn, I was so happy. Then came the strike. Now don't get me wrong. I want this strike. We need that extra money to live like human beings. But what a time for a kid to come, huh?"

There was something else, too. The constant worry about getting enough stuff for the baby was making his wife nervous and when he'd try to calm her down, he'd get nervous too. Then the baby would start crying and his mother-in-law would pitch in something. . . .

"Sometimes I feel like blowing my top, just exploding," Tennelli continued. "You know, I haven't paid my rent for two months, not since the strike started. If I had to, then it would be goodbye Charlie for me. I haven't even bought a newspaper because three cents is three cents. And we never go visiting any more because the carfare would buy milk for the baby. So I feel like a rat when I buy a few butts for a nickel, and I used to smoke a couple packs a day.

"Clothes? Are you kidding? Jesus, look at this," he said, showing how torn his cuffs were. "The hell with clothes. I'm talking about money for bread."

He kept staring at his torn cuffs and then he spoke pleadingly. "What am I supposed to do when worse comes to worst? Stick up a bank?" He tried to smile and couldn't. "The sign I carried on the picket line. Know what it said? It said, 'We fought for freedom and democracy and this is what we got.' "

Outside at the corner, you could see the small semicircle of pickets walking quickly to keep warm. Watching them from across the street was a policeman with his collar turned up, rubbing his hands.

Down the block, in the larger office of the headquarters of Local 410, Dave Thomas was sitting at a desk, working over some papers. The radio was tuned into some female quartet, but nobody in the room was listening.

Thomas, an ex-3rd Division marine, home from Saipan, was chairman of the union's veterans committee. The first thing he talked about was the demonstration that five hundred of the union's veterans had at the state capitol the week before.

"All we wanted to do was to tell the Governor how much we needed the unemployment compensation, not for ourselves so much, but for our wives and kids and old folks," Thomas explained. "But he wouldn't even see our committee. A Governor is supposed to be an elected servant of the people, a guy you're supposed to be able to see any time you want to, isn't he?"

Thomas' voice got bitter. "Well, the payoff is that the company's representative went down to see the Governor the week afterwards and got right in. How do you like that?"

Something just as bad was the way the people reacted to the five hundred vets marching around the capitol with their signs. No passer-by said anything to them; few even stopped to stare.

"They just ignored us," Thomas went on quietly. "I guess that's worse than anything. Even if they had booed, it might have been better. At least we'd know they were noticing us. But making believe we weren't there . . . that hurt."

One of the girls interrupted to ask where the postcards were. The subject switched to food and Thomas remarked that the welfare people had already started paying the milk bill for his two kids; the only three meals they could afford at home were frankfurters, hamburgers and spaghetti, and they were running short on all of them.

"It's the same old story," he continued. "All that crap the company sent us overseas, how they would really take care of us when we got home. Well, they really did. Now they're just saying, 'I've got mine, hooray for me, the hell with you.' And that vice-chancellor in Newark saying that veterans on the picket line are nothing more than Hitler's storm troopers. Sometimes I have to keep reminding myself that this is really the United States of America."

Thomas looked skeptically at my note-taking. "I told some of this stuff to a New York reporter last week," he said. "Only it never got into print. I guess newspapers don't like to print stories about how strikers live on almost nothing. I tell you, they've forgotten about us. Nobody cares any more." He smiled thinly. "Pardon me," he added, "but I don't think this will get printed either."

Several people walked in then, including Bill Doull, veterans counselor at the union's welfare section. He admitted that fewer than twenty veterans had applied for welfare relief.

"I'm not sure why that is," he said, "because veterans here are just like any other workers, just as typical. Yet when a vet comes around to us, we know that he's really down and out— no bonds, no savings, no nothing. And the only ones we ever get are the ones with kids."

The first thing he tells them is that union welfare isn't charity because they paid for it in dues. Then he makes them even more comfortable by telling them that he himself is getting welfare relief.

"Before I applied, though, I used up all the money I had saved to buy a car," said Doull. "I used to dream about that car in the Army, the one thing I really wanted. Oh, well. . . ."

Back in the basement, Hull had just finished an inventory of another food contribution. "I forgot to tell you," he started out, "that if the company thinks they're going to break this union by keeping us out longer, then they're crazy. This is the first strike this union has had since it got started in 1937 and for the first time the workers are realizing that they're all tied up together on one side of the fence, that they've got to stick together. This union has never been stronger than it is now."

When he finished, he brought me to another part of the cellar where a man and several boys were busy wrapping papers. The man's name was Betts, a former councilman who owned the stationery store upstairs. He had donated the use of this cellar to the union.

"It's the least I could do," Betts said. "If you needed help and you came to me and I could help you, then I would, that's all. We're all human beings, aren't we? What's everything all about if people won't help each other? Or am I crazy?"

To those soldiers who had never thought about it much, the war's meaning was beginning to sink in deep.

"You mean they took all these people and worked them like slaves? I used to think it was just a lot of propaganda back home."

Soon to come were more of the same, piled up thick. Soon to come were the concentration camps, the huge piles of naked, stinking, beaten bodies of prisoners piled up like cordwood, the living dead with skin so tight over the gaping bones that you expected it to crack when they bent over. Soon to come were the walls of torture chambers covered with the imprints of feet which had kicked and kicked before death finally came. And the stories, the incredible stories which you didn't believe until they took off their clothes and showed you. People's behinds beaten into rawness by big clubs and then the wounds cut open and salt rubbed in. People whipped like dogs would never be whipped. People burned alive, women's breasts cut off, men hung by their testicles. How many millions of people, how many millions of stories?

Soldiers who never knew what fascism really was, knew it now.

12

THE WAR ISN'T OVER YET

MAYBE it was too hot to fight fascism that night. Standing sweaty in a crowd listening to speeches when you could be home sitting beside a fan with your shoes off.

But down at St. Louis' Soldier Memorial, a couple hundred people did come. The orange sunset disappeared into thick black clouds while the small crowd waited quietly, some sitting on the steps, the rest standing. A sprinkling of Negroes, some Nisei, a few Panama hats, a scattered handful of curious bums. But mostly, they were anybody.

Young, anxious Douglas McCleod of the American Veterans Committee, the meeting chairman, spoke without notes, the emotion spilling quickly from inside of him. That burning cross in a St. Louis playground for Negro children was all tied up with the fascist philosophy of Gerald L. K. Smith, he said. So why should the city of St. Louis make its civic auditorium available to Smith to preach his fascist hate? It was a hate-thy-neighbor fascism that wrecked Europe and would wreck us if we didn't stop it.

A young man with a hearing aid moved closer to the speaker. Two tense-faced young Negroes nodded their heads, almost in rhythm.

"But he'll never be able to do that in our country," finished McCleod.

No applause yet. The crowd's quiet was almost eerie. And the fast-growing darkness was punctured only by the sudden flash of a photographer's bulb.

People like Gerald L. K. Smith were a good thing, began the next speaker, the Reverend Charles Wilson of the Citizens' Council for Democracy. They were good for us because they made us think, made us realize that you can't call Smith a crackpot and let it go at that. People laughed at Hitler once. The only thing to do was to fight fascism here and now. In St. Louis, he said, there was not only the problem of too many little rats, but of big ones. . . . "I'm talking about Gerald Smith's meeting at our civic auditorium the day after to-morrow."

A sudden clap of thunder and the crowd turned to look up. You could hear the foghorns sobbing on the Mississippi. The lights inside the Memorial Building flicked on and you could see the words above the columns: "TO OUR SOLDIER DEAD."

"Anybody who thinks the war is over is living in a dream world," Mr. Wilson continued. "The fascists are still among us."

It was early yet. Still an hour before Smith's speakers would start inside. But the cops were already thick in the street. Almost three hundred of them. Plus police cars, wagons, squad cars, motorcycles, plainclothesmen.

At the main ticket entrance, several dozen police were lined shoulder to shoulder on both sides of the canopy. A reporter quipped that all they needed were sabers and they could have a military wedding. But nobody laughed; it wasn't funny. You could feel everyone's tenseness, the waiting for trouble.

Some of the audience started arriving, a small parade of old women without wedding rings, women with small, sour, wrin-

kled faces, "pickled in the vinegar of their own disillusion-
ment." Coming here for what? To prove they weren't dead,
that they could still hate?

"Looks like the Townsend Plan, doesn't it?"

Then suddenly five Negroes walked toward the entrance
with their tickets in their hands. But the blond-haired man
with the thin lips hardly glanced at their tickets. "These tickets
are counterfeit, officer," he said to the nearest policeman.
"These people can't come in." Obediently, the cop motioned
to other cops near-by, and the photographers got their cameras
set, waiting for trouble. But there was no trouble.

Another man, without a ticket, just stood there and talked
loudly. "So much police protection for Gerald Smith and
hardly any for Bob Hope last night. Maybe Smith is funnier
than Hope." His smile faded and his voice grew bitter. "But I
don't think so."

Some more audience. A policeman recognized an old friend
among the ticket-holders, "Hello George, how come your
wife's not with you here tonight?"

Then a group of veterans, all with their discharge buttons
and their tickets. But the woman next to the collector spoke up
loudly, "Don't let them in. I recognize one of them. He was
on that picket line."

Again the police crowded in quickly, pushing the veterans
back, ordering, "Come on, get back there."

"But, officer, we've all got tickets."

"You heard me, move along."

The street filled with people now. Some plainclothesmen
edged in hurriedly. More cops pushed in from the sides.

"Hey, officer, why don't you let Smith form his own goon
squad?"

"Which side are you on anyway, the people's or the
fascists'?"

"Know what Mayor Kaufman's secretary told me over the phone today? She couldn't understand why we were protesting about Smith because he was no worse than Father Coughlin and everybody knew that Coughlin was all right."

"You cops can stop shoving—we're moving. . . ."

Then, suddenly, you saw the beginning.

A cop sneaked behind the loudest-talking veteran and swung a roundhouse blow to his head. Turning around swinging, the vet was grabbed, pulled to the fringe of the crowd, a dozen cops closing him in a circle, their arms slugging. Through their legs, you could see the vet's bloodied body on the pavement, his hands covering his face. The twisted look of hate on the police captain's face as he kicked the body again and again.

And suddenly the crowd swells and swerves and you're no longer a bystander; you're in the middle of it. A woman's screaming voice, "Don't hit my brother. . . . Leave my brother alone. . . ." A cop only three feet away from you straight-arming a frightened blonde woman. On the steps, a small man yelling. "This isn't democracy, this is fascism," until three cops turn off to get him, twist his arm, throw him into the patrol wagon. Another circle of cops beating up someone else, throwing his body into a squad car, with a cop hitting the body once more for good measure. . . . The thin, shrill, crying voice of a woman, "Let me get to my husband. . . . I want to be with my husband . . ." and forcing herself into the squad car. In the center of the crowd, a strong voice shouting, "I remember when fifty cops threw down their badges rather than fight for fascism!" An old Negro woman squeezed in the middle of everything, screeching, "Let me out of here. . . . Let me out of here . . ."

And on the near-by street corner, a small, elderly woman, blind and deaf to everything, droning loudly, "Peanuts only five cents. . . . Get your peanuts right here, folks."

Up on the auditorium's first-floor balcony, eight men from Smith's audience had come out to watch the show. To them it was funnier than Bob Hope. They laughed and poked each other when the screaming woman forced herself into the squad car to be with her husband. They were having a wonderful time.

The cops dragged, pulled, and carried one man after another into the police wagon. Just before it pulled away, somebody inside broke out with, "Every man inside here is a veteran . . . every man inside here is a veteran. . . . Is this what we fought fascism for?"

Repeating it over and over again, almost chanting it, until it was only an echo.

Then quiet again. The people had all moved across the street to the small park. The front of the auditorium was now almost solid with police. A woman crossed the street and walked slowly down the block facing the police, yelling in a high-pitched, tearful voice almost ready to break, "Doesn't it seem funny to arrest the veterans . . . doesn't it seem funny?"

The police just stood there, still as stone, not looking at each other, their eyes following the single woman who walked the full length of the block yelling her question, then recrossed the street to the park.

Meanwhile, some more Smith audience. A large group of expensively dressed women laughing gayly as if this were a social tea or a bridge party or a class reunion. Another parade of old people with empty faces, and some young people with bitter faces, and the tough, weather-beaten faces of husky farmers. Somewhere in between them, the sad, lonely face of a young girl carrying her baby. You hoped the ticket collector would turn her away, but he didn't.

It was a game you played: this guy will get in, that one won't.

Is there such a thing as a fascist face?

"It's all right, folks. You don't need any tickets. You can come right in."

The whispering conversation of some reporters. "Did you see that cop slug the guy from behind? I saw the whole thing."

"So what. You're not going to put that in your story, are you?"

And a policeman arriving late on the scene, being greeted by his buddies, "Say, Joe, you missed all the fun."

Quiet again. Then out of the quiet the loud voice of an army sergeant barking, "Hut, two, three four. . . . Hut, two, three, four. . . . Hut. . . . Hut. Dress it up. . . ."

The people marched in a single file across the street, down the block of the auditorium, circled to form a picket line. The people: veterans still in uniform, a tiny hunchbacked lady, a toothless old man standing straight and smiling, college girls, women with their husbands, black and white and yellow, Christian and Jew, a heavy old woman walking slowly. . . .

"Mama, you don't have to walk with us. You can sit on a park bench and watch us. . . ."

"Let me alone. I want to walk with you. . . ."

Hut, two, three, four . . . hut . . . hut . . .

One of the reporters looked at his watch. "Say, it's time to go in and listen to Smith. Coming?"

"Me? I'd rather go home and puke in my own toilet."

"Sure, there were lots of bodies we never identified. You know what a direct hit by a shell does to a guy. Or a mine. Or a solid hit with a grenade even. Sometimes all we have is a leg or a hunk of arm," said T/Sgt. Donald Haguall, of the 48th Quartermaster Graves Registration.

"The ones that stink the worst are the guys who got internal wounds and are dead about three weeks with the blood staying inside and rotting; when you move the body the blood comes out of the nose and mouth. Then some of them bloat up in the sun, they bloat up so big that they bust the buttons and then they get blue and the skin peels. They don't all get blue, some of them get black.

"But they all stink. There's only one stink and that's it. You never get used to it, either. As long as you live, you never get used to it. And after a while, the stink gets in your clothes and you can taste it in your mouth. If you think about it too much, you go to Section 8.

"You know what I think? I think maybe if every civilian in the world could smell the stink of death for an hour or even ten minutes, then I think we wouldn't have any more wars. What do you think?"

13

WHERE IS HOME?

A SOLDIER and his girl were swaying in a half-dance, their bodies bending to the rhythm of a soft, sweet jazz, their feet shuffling just slightly. In the back of the room some soldiers were bunched in a semicircle, sipping cokes and swapping stories. Occasionally, one of them would break out into a loud, sharp laugh and keep laughing until the others joined in. Sitting at the tables were some serious-faced couples concentrating on gin rummy.

At the desk near the door, right next to a USO sign, the thin girl in the bright dress smiled when she said, "It's kinda dead around here now. You should have come yesterday. We had a big dance yesterday." She told how good the band was and how big the crowd was and that there were almost as many veterans around as there were soldiers.

"That's because these boys here in Washington just don't have too many other places to get together," she said. "This isn't the Old South, but it's still a long way from New York City, and a Negro is still a Negro."

She bit her lip when she said that, as if she were trying to stop herself from talking too much.

One of the gin-rummy games broke up and a slim, young-looking civilian detached himself from the group, sat down on the sofa, picked up a copy of *Popular Science* and started thumbing through it slowly.

"Look at him," said the girl at the desk. "That's Chester Whiteside. He's been out of the Army since August and he still comes here pretty regularly. He's lonely."

A few minutes later, Chester was spilling out why he was lonely. It was because he left his wife down in North Carolina teaching school while he came home to Washington to try to find a job until the college term started. Only he couldn't find a job. He was a qualified clerk and there was supposed to be a shortage of clerks and he had looked everywhere but nobody seemed to want him. Still, he wasn't surprised. He had expected it, he said. He had expected a lot of things.

"You hear a lot of stuff about how homesick the overseas American soldier is for the good old U.S.A.," he said. "But you don't hear much of that from the Negro soldier. Not the ones in Europe. Anyway, not the ones I know, not the ones in the 41st Engineers. Hell, why should they be homesick? Homesick for Jim Crow, for poll taxes and segregated slums? Homesick for lynchings and race riots?"

He brooded about that for a minute and then he spoke up softly as if he were telling secrets. "I don't know if you ever heard about some of the race riots we had in Europe. The Army kept it quiet, I guess. Hitler would have loved to hear about it. Well, we had one of them in Marseilles, a small one. They tried to kill a few of our boys because they were dancing with white French girls. The girls never even thought about it being something special. To them, we were just people, human beings. But to some of the white soldiers, we were just niggers. I'll never forget the one who yelled, 'Just wait until the war's over, we'll know how to take care of you nigger bastards.'

"Well," said Chester, still softly, "the war's over."

Somebody turned up the radio's volume control. It was a sugary-voiced crooner singing "Embraceable You" and some of the couples at the food counter joined in, humming loudly.

Chester was still in Marseilles. "As I said before," he continued, "some of the riots weren't so small. A lot of boys got hurt, some got killed. Our boys knew what was coming up. You'd have to be deaf, dumb and blind not to."

There was a long moment of thick quiet and then Chester's voice sounded strained. "Have you ever been to a lynching?"

He seemed to empty himself into the sofa's softness, leaning his head back, staring at the ceiling, speaking slowly as if he were having a tough time pulling things out of his memory.

"It was in a little town called Shelbyville, in Tennessee, a long time ago," he said. "I can still see the teacher running into our class and telling all us colored kids to hurry home and stay home. That's all she said and none of us knew what was the matter, but the fear in the teacher's eyes was like a fever. I remember how we all looked at each other and a few kids started to cry and then we all raced out of the room. Suddenly there were white kids all around us throwing rocks and yelling dirty names, and I remember running so fast that I thought my heart would bust wide open. I was seven years old."

The radio crooner had changed his mood. He was singing a rapid-running song with tricky words about South America and love. One girl was shaking to the rhythm of it and two others were watching her, giggling.

Chester was tearing small pieces off the back cover of the copy of *Popular Science*.

"We never left our house for three full days," he said. "I remember all the noise outside and then the sudden quiet, and I remember how scared I always was and how my mother kept praying all the time.

"I never did get the whole story. I know they burned down the courthouse to grab the colored boy out of jail. He was only nineteen. I still don't know what he was supposed to have done."

He looked at the torn cover of the magazine without seeming to see it and then tossed it on the table. "That was December 25, 1928. Isn't it funny the way a date sticks in your mind sometimes? Isn't it really funny?"

He hunched over in his seat, folding his hands, cracking his knuckles. Then, suddenly, his voice snapped out sharp and bitter. "We had white officers in our outfit," he said. "Mostly Southern whites. They hated us and we hated them. The officers who were sympathetic didn't last long; they got transferred out in a hurry.

"You ought to hear the orientation talks they gave us. The way they talked, democracy and segregation meant the same thing. Only they never ever let it go at that. Some of the men got kicked and slapped and cursed and shoved around like scummy dirt—and what the hell could you do?"

Chester opened his fists and wiggled his fingers.

"But there's a limit to how much you can push people around," he said, speaking softly again. "Some guys can only take so much. Then they crack. There was one guy who started a one-man riot. He killed an officer and before they hunted him down, he wounded a couple more."

Chester looked around the room until he saw a soldier with a Purple Heart talking seriously with a petite, pretty girl.

"See that guy," said Chester. "He knows how to shoot a rifle now. If somebody ever shoots at him sometime, maybe he'll shoot back. You get sick and tired of running away all the time."

They had also been sick and tired of hearing white soldiers throw up to them the fact that there were so few Negroes in

combat, he said. The way they talked, you'd think the Negro
had something to say about what he did or where he went
in the Army. It was in Antwerp that Chester's outfit first heard
about the Army finally deciding to train Negroes as infantry-
men. They were to fight in platoons, alongside white units.
Nobody had to volunteer if he didn't want to. But in Chester's
company of 160, 72 volunteered, some of them offering to take
busts from master sergeant to private. But only seven were
selected. Three of the seven later got Silver Stars for excep-
tional gallantry in action.

"I don't know why we volunteered in the first place," said
Chester. "Just to show the world that we were willing to fight,
even though most of us didn't have much to fight for."

"A few days ago, I bumped into one of those seven guys,"
said Chester. "He had all kinds of ribbons but he was bitter
as hell. He said he had just come back from the South and it
didn't seem to make any difference if you fought or you didn't
fight; he was still only a black boy."

Chester himself was hopeful when he first came home. They
had shipped him to a camp in Wilmington and black and
white ate in the same mess hall, slept in the same barracks.
The way everybody acted, it seemed as if it had always been
that way.

It all seemed almost worth while—the stinking wet heat of
Liberia and Dakar, the D-day landing in Oran, all those hos-
pitals and airfields they built in Tunisia, Sicily, Sardinia,
Corsica, then the D-day landing at Red Beach in St. Tropez.
Three years and three months of it.

Then came Fort Bragg and Jim Crow.

It was Jim Crow on the bus, too—an old bus on a bumpy
road, but Chester was singing happy. His 118 points had
earned him a discharge and he was going to see his Myrtle.

"Myrtle's my wonderful wife," Chester explained, smiling

for the first time. "We got married ten days before I went overseas."

He warmed himself in that; then suddenly he stopped smiling and told about the bus trip. The bus was full when a white man got on, looked around and then whispered something to the bus driver. Then the bus driver got up, looked back at the Jim Crow seats, and pointing to Chester, told him to get up and stand. "No nigger is going to sit in my bus while a white man is standing," the bus driver had said loudly.

Rather than stand in the bus, Chester got out and walked. It was sixteen miles to the nearest town.

"I had a lot of time to think," he said. "I had a helluva lot of time to think. . . ."

The crooner had changed into a quiz show and a tall soldier quickly went over and fiddled with the dials until he got a brassy band bouncing out some jive. One couple automatically started a fast Lindy hop but the girl stopped in the middle of a twirl and laughed. "There's not enough room with all these tables," she said.

"Myrtle and I are going to Liberia," said Chester quietly. "We're going as soon as we can, as soon as I can finish this mortician's course." He smiled faintly. "I'll be the only mortician in Liberia."

He told about how he was the first American Negro soldier to land in Liberia back in May, 1942, and how he got acquainted with the Liberian President, and how the country was just aching for improvement, with almost ten million uneducated people who didn't even know the fundamentals of sanitation.

"Myrtle and I can do some good there," he said, "and then maybe when we're lots older, we'll go to France. Have you ever been to France?" he asked. "France is wonderful. Over there they practice the tolerance that America only preaches.

"Myrtle will love France," he said, smiling again. "The closest Myrtle ever got to democracy was here in Washington. She just couldn't get over the fact that there actually weren't any Jim Crow seats on the trolley cars. Can you imagine how she'll feel in France? Can you just imagine?"

"I'm so glad we're going," he said. "It would have been different if I found America different. I didn't expect any revolutionary changes in the attitude toward Negroes. All I wanted was a sign in the wind, just the smallest sign that things were getting better instead of worse. If Congress had only passed an anti-lynch law or a permanent F.E.P.C., something, anything. . . ."

A heavy-set girl turned off the radio and announced in a high voice that they were starting a bingo game.

"Maybe Myrtle and I are doing the wrong thing," he said, rubbing his hands nervously. "Maybe we should stay here and stick it out and maybe, God knows, our kids might someday be treated like first-class Americans instead of third-class dirt.

"But I guess we're selfish; we don't want to wait that long. In fact we'll probably give up our American citizenship and become French citizens, like a lot of my friends are doing.

"You see," he said quietly, stretching out his words, "it isn't a question whether Myrtle and I are American citizens or French citizens; it's whether or not we're human beings."

The wet cold had crept inside their clothes several days before, when they first came up to this OP. It was the misery of the numbing, dirty dampness that first made them start talking about soaking in warm baths and climbing in between soft white sheets. Then the talk shifted to Christmas and good food and how they'd give their right arms if they could only be home for Christmas.

One guy said he had a kid he had never seen because his picture hadn't come yet and he felt pretty bad because he wasn't able to send him a present; another guy said that he always went home for Christmas, that this was the first Christmas he couldn't make it, and his folks must be terrible lonely; and the third guy said that if he had one wish now he would wish that he could be back home in bed with his wife.

They said all this as they stood around a small fire, wet and dirty, cold, hungry, miserable and full of hurting emptiness. Three more guys came up later to relieve them. When one guy said "Merry Christmas," the three guys looked surprised and one of them said slowly, "We thought tomorrow was Christmas."

14

HOME TO NORTH PLATTE

North Platte's White Horse Bar was almost empty when the bartender made a short speech about how there was a new tone to the town. It was because of all the veterans coming home, he said. More noise, more parties, more girls dressed prettier, more people laughing in the street. It was different than it used to be, he said.

Months ago, when the soldiers got discharged in driblets, he remembered how they wandered into the bar one at a time, looking lonely. Some of them would have a few quick drinks and leave. But every once in a while, one of them would insist on buying him a drink, just to have somebody to talk to. And the first thing he would say would almost always be, "Jeezus, I walked all around town and I hardly know anybody any more."

Now they rushed in, a lot of them at a time, still all excited, some of them slapping each other on the back and talking loudly without knowing it. He seldom heard them talk about the war, though. He thought it was probably because everybody figured that maybe somebody else in the crowd saw more combat than he did.

But if there were only two of them, just a couple of buddies, then they talked about everything, bringing themselves up-to-date on when they were where, and what the women were like.

"Of course," said the bartender, "none of them would tell me any stories about the war." He picked up a German helmet and pretended to examine the signatures scrawled on it. "They don't want to hurt my feelings," he said. "I'm a 4-F."

But he had talked to them about other things. No, he hadn't heard them bitch much, except, of course, about the housing situation.

Several doors away, in the Chamber of Commerce office, a serious-faced, deep-voiced young man was trying to explain why some of the fifteen thousand people in this town were unsuccessfully hunting for places to live. He told how the Union Pacific was the biggest boss in town, handing out a weekly payroll of two thousand checks. Then, when the war pulled out their workers, other people moved into North Platte from other towns to get the railroad jobs. And now they weren't moving; they liked it here.

So far, the city's only solution was to get an allotment of eighty trailer homes from the federal government. But nobody had the slightest idea when they would be delivered. Nobody knew when the privately purchased prefabricated homes were coming either. And nobody had the vaguest notion as to how long it would be before construction materials would be available for building regular homes.

There was another headache, too, though, the job headache. Since there were no industries in town, the thing he had been recommending to business-minded veterans was for them to open a few more retail stores, maybe a lithography plant, and certainly some more eating places. Right now, you couldn't even get a malted milk in town after seven o'clock at night.

About individual jobs for veterans, well, he didn't know for sure. "You ought to see the USES about that," he said.

The gray-haired USES manager laughed away the job worry. He said that there were plenty of jobs, and if the vet couldn't find any in North Platte, don't forget there was still the rest of Lincoln County. And Lincoln was the second biggest county in Nebraska.

What kind of jobs? Why, only this morning, he got six unsolicited offers for veterans in on-the-job training. That was the government's offer to supplement a certain amount of wages for veterans learning new trades. The wages had ranged from twenty-five to forty-five dollars a week and they had placed forty-five men in jobs like that, and there would be lots more.

Of course, there was a limit. Pretty soon, there might be an unemployment lag, he said. A few companies already had canceled their job offers. And after the veterans here picked off all the good jobs, there wouldn't be too much for the others to choose from. But all this was just temporary, he said. Things would start humming soon. Road construction, lots of new buildings, things like that. He wasn't at all worried. North Platte would take care of its own. "If you want to see what the North Platte people do for servicemen, why don't you go down to the canteen?" he said.

The canteen, a big room at the railroad station, had a long row of tables packed with all kinds of delicious-looking home-cooked food. On the side was a sign, "Today's Specialty—Hot Turkey Sandwiches." Behind the tables, a large group of motherly-looking women were trading talk, waiting for customers.

Sitting behind the reception desk, a pretty girl smiled automatically. They sometimes served almost eight thousand servicemen a day, she said, and all of it was absolutely free. There had been all kinds of write-ups about it in different magazines and they all said it was one of the best service canteens in the country.

"And it really is," said the pretty girl seriously.

Lots of soldiers had told her personally that if the rest of the people in town were as nice as the people in the canteen, then they were going to move here after the war. "And I wouldn't be surprised if they mean it, too," she said.

Most of her own boy friends hadn't been discharged yet and she hadn't talked to any other veterans about how they felt, but she couldn't imagine any veteran having any complaints about North Platte. "Because it's just the same now as it always was," she said.

An elderly woman standing near the entrance suddenly let loose a small squeal of delight. "I see a train coming," she said excitedly. Some more women quickly clustered around the entrance. "Get ready, girls," one said, and they all stopped their talk and moved behind their food tables, brushing away imaginary dust.

At a small café across the street, the healthy-looking waitress laughed when she said, "Oh yeah, sure, I've been dating a lot of veterans lately. They're all ages, from twenty to forty."

"Most of them aren't too happy, either," she said. "You know how that song goes . . . how you gonna keep 'em down on the farm after they've seen Paree? Well, that's it. Only most of these guys have seen New York and L.A. and Frisco and lots of other big places like that. So now North Platte seems awful little and awful dead."

There just weren't too many places in town where you could go and have yourself a big time, she said. There was the small Arrowhead and another new one called Joe's Place, also on the outskirts of town. Then there was a club in town, X Servicemen, but it was mostly a crowded gambling joint. And that's all there was.

But it was more than that, she said. In the first place, you couldn't find anywhere to live in town and in the second place the returning vets she knew were kinda particular about what job they took. She could hardly blame them about that, because it costs so much more to live now than it used to.

Take her brother, for example. He made three hundred a month as a fighter pilot during the war. Now he's been sitting around for four months doing nothing because the best job offer he got was thirty a week.

"He's going to California," she said. "He doesn't know what he's going to do there, but he's going anyway. There's lots of others here like him, too."

Meanwhile, it was nice having all these men back in town again. During the war there was never enough men to go around, she said. "Besides, I'm not the type to go in for sewing clubs."

Rus Langford, who runs a big wholesale grocery company, listened to the story about the fighter pilot and shook his head.

"What kind of jobs can you give them?" he asked. "Most of them just got a high-school diploma and never learned a trade. They can't even get a job flying now, because pilots are a dime a dozen."

He told how few good jobs there were to offer in town and how a lieutenant colonel was coming back to his old route, delivering mail. Then he told how the Union Pacific just announced that it was going to lay off twenty-five men and it was almost dead sure that most of them would be recently hired veterans who didn't have any seniority. And the longer the veteran waited before job-hunting, the fewer the jobs and the stiffer the competition.

The man with Langford, a guy named Joe who worked in the radio station, broke in to describe the vets in town who didn't have to worry about a future to fit into. They were the rich kids who could always depend on mama and papa, the farm boys who could always go back to the farm, and the athletes who could go back to any college they wanted to.

Joe also had a private suggestion that maybe a lot of vets who couldn't find the jobs and homes they wanted might re-enlist.

The rested-looking lieutenant at the Army Recruiting Station in town admitted that business wasn't too good. And there were all these advantages a re-enlisting veteran got, he said. There was the ninety-day furlough right off the bat and you could keep your old rating and in sixteen or seventeen years you could retire. Besides that, the money you made in the Army, counting room and board, was probably more than you could make on the outside.

How many re-enlistments from North Platte so far? Well, he didn't know exactly, he would have to look through his file.

"I guess we only have two," he said, after thumbing through some cards.

Business was also slow in the judge's office, according to the middle-aged secretary. And she just couldn't understand it either, she said. She thought that a lot of veterans would come in and get married right after they got home. But they didn't. The marriage rate was just about the same as last year, slow. Funny part about it was that there were almost as many divorces in the last year as there were marriages. About the marriages, she had been talking it over with a friend and they had decided that the reason people weren't getting married was because they couldn't find a place to live.

Downstairs, the white-haired county farm agent said he had been busy, that a lot of veterans had been up to see him recently. Most of them wanted to buy their own farms.

"But I told them all not to," he said. "I told them that farms today cost 25 to 50 per cent more than they ever did and if they just waited a year or two, then the price would come down. Why? Because there's nothing to hold them up anymore; the war's over."

It was getting dark outside and most of the stores were closing for the night. The big Hawes Pool Room was still full of customers, mostly high-school kids and a sprinkling of soldiers. Across the street, facing the railroad station, the Alamo, "the bar that Buffalo Bill drank over," was full of the usual transients getting a drink in between trains.

At the edge of the bar, two sober soldiers drinking beer were talking about North Platte. "Somebody told me that this wasn't really Buffalo Bill's home town," said the taller one.

The other just nodded. "What's the difference?" he said. "This is still the kind of town I like. Look how peaceful it is. Plenty of fresh air, lots of quiet and friendly people, and nobody worries about anything much. Just normal living. When I get married, I'm gonna move to a town just like this and buy me a small house and open up a store and raise kids. This is for me."

The taller soldier killed his beer, thought it over and shrugged his shoulders. "I'll still take Brooklyn," he said.

What the paratroopers said was: "If this is war, we want more."
They said it softly, though, because up in the cold snow of
the foggy mountains, patrols had a way of going out and never
coming back. It was an eerie war, too.

But what they were talking about was Nice itself, sitting
within shellfire range of the front, with its neon lights blazing,
its modern little nightclubs filled with real Scotch whiskey
and beautiful women dressed in soft silk, and hot pianos beating out boogie woogie just like in Café Society Downtown in
Greenwich Village.

Occasionally the glass in the windows shivered from the
near-by naval shelling, but the beautiful babes weren't paying
any attention and neither was the pianist, and neither was the
bartender. But then one of the paratroopers looked at his watch
and said, "Well, this has to be the last drink because I have
to go on patrol pretty soon."

15

IS IT ASKING TOO MUCH?

I T'S ONE of those streets on Detroit's West Side that sits
alongside the railroad tracks, a long row of dingy, white,
wooden houses, mostly carbon copies. Joe Wadrzyk and his
wife live at 9516 Graham Street, the only house in the block
with an iron fence around it. They live upstairs in four, small,
neatly kept rooms.

"This place isn't as nice as the one we used to live in before
I went into the Army," said Joe, who is short, heavy-set, slow-
talking. "We used to live in a five-room house all by ourselves,"
he said, wiping his glasses. "But that used to cost us thirty-
five bucks a month. That's a lot of money, I guess." He took
a quick look around the small living room. "We only pay
twenty a month for this place."

The screeching noise of a fast-moving train drowned out
the conversation and the building trembled. "It sure makes
a helluva racket, don't it?" he remarked.

He was staring out of the window at the disappearing train
as he continued. "You know, things are sure a lot different
back here than I thought they'd be. Over in Germany, I sorta
had the bright idea that all I had to do was to come home and
get fat and rich."

His wife's loud laugh came from the kitchen. "Maybe you

got a little fat, Joe," she called in. "But you sure didn't get rich."

Joe pretended not to hear. "I got my first paycheck this week," he said, "and you know what I got? I got thirty-nine ninety and by the time they sliced off the dough for taxes and insurance, I had thirty-four bucks left to take home. Can you imagine that? Thirty-four bucks a week, only fourteen more than when I started as a messenger boy for General Motors twenty-two years ago. Isn't that a laugh? It's like starting all over again now."

"And you're not a spring chicken any more," said his wife softly, sitting down in the living room. She was a round-faced, husky woman with a pleasant smile, only she wasn't smiling now.

"No," Joe said slowly, "I'm not a spring chicken any more."

Joe's wife unconsciously folded and unfolded her hands. "Thirty-four dollars a week used to be good money, Joe," she said cheerfully. "When we got married five years ago, it was wonderful money."

She retold everything they had bought with his old salary—all the new furniture, the clothes, the car.

"But what can you buy with it now?" asked Joe. "It goes like that," and he snapped his fingers. "Before the war we'd go shopping on a Saturday and we'd buy all the groceries we needed for a whole week for only five bucks," he said. "Now it costs us at least fifteen a week for food alone, sometimes even twenty."

He picked up the newspaper and then threw it down. "Hell, even the paper costs a nickel now."

Then he picked up the paper again and looked at the head-lines. "And if you read all the papers," he said, "you'd think that all us workers are just a bunch of Reds if we go out on strike to try to get 30 per cent more wages. Me, I'm a registered Democrat and twelve bucks more a week isn't gonna make me a millionaire."

Joe remembered something and laughed.

"I guess if I had talked like this about strikes and wages when I was up front in France with my old outfit, I'll bet sure as hell some guy would have cut me down with a machine gun." Then he smiled. "Come to think of it," he said sheepishly, "the way I used to feel then, I might have pulled the trigger on myself."

When Joe was drafted, the newspapers were still splashing every strike all over their front pages. But as a worker and a union member, he figured that most of the stuff was exaggerated hot air. When some of his GI buddies started talking about "slapping those striking bastards into the Army," Joe even tried arguing with them, but he never seemed to convince anybody.

By the time his outfit was in a staging area in England, sweating out the invasion of Europe, the talk about strikes had become more intense. Stuff like this:

"How do you like that? Another strike back home. What do those striking sons-of-bitches want now? Do they want blood? Those 4-F bastards don't even know there's a war on. They're back home living the life of Riley, making all the dough, buying new clothes and beautiful cars, going to night clubs, sleeping with our women. Why don't they bring those bastards over here and stick them in on the invasion and let us go home?"

That was common talk. Those who kept quiet agreed with at least some of it.

Even Pfc. Joseph Wadrzyk.

Joe was thirty-nine years old and he was a rifleman in an infantry outfit and maybe he was going to die, and nobody wants to die.

"When you're tired and mad and scared like that," explained Joe apologetically, "then it's tough to think straight. Besides it seemed like every time I picked up a paper or turned on a radio, there was another strike going on. It just seemed like too much, as if 90 per cent of the workers in America were out on strike."

Several weeks later, Joe was sweating out a mortar barrage in a hole behind a hedgerow in France alongside the rest of the second squad of the second platoon of Company I, 357th Regiment, 90th Division. The hole was Joe's bedroom, kitchen, and toilet, and the only time he left it was when he went on night patrol.

In the filth, the fear, and the loneliness of the hedgerow war, America was a million miles away, a dream country of cake and ice cream, white sheets, hot baths, and beautiful women. Everybody who was lucky enough to be there should be so thankful for it that he would work seven days and seven nights a week for nothing, and anybody who wanted to strike should be lined up against the wall and be shot, lynched, tarred and feathered, and hung by his testicles where everybody could see him.

That's what most front-line soldiers thought, almost what Joe was beginning to think. It was envy and ignorance and fear all mixed up. But the big thing was that there was nobody around to tell them different.

There was nobody to tell them that if all the workers back home were on strike, then who do you think was producing all the ships, planes, tanks and guns; there was nobody to give them the stark facts and figures about strikes, that they amounted to less than one-tenth of one per cent, and even those were just as much the fault of management as of labor; there was nobody to explain to them the relationship between prices and wages, to tell them that workers working overtime were too tired to go to night clubs, that there weren't any new cars to buy during wartime; there was nobody to ask them, "If you want to lynch the workers of America, then what the hell are you fighting for?"

Joe learned all these things after he was liberated from a German prison camp near Munich.

His first lesson came when his wife went down to Miami with him while he waited for reassignment. Joe felt rich because he had four hundred dollars in accumulated back pay.

"And I just couldn't understand it," he said. "We didn't go to any night clubs or shows or anything like that. I didn't even buy any new clothes. Just normal, ordinary, everyday living. But before we knew it we were almost broke."

Joe's second lesson was when he came home after his discharge. He met up with some of his old buddies who had worked with General Motors during the war and he was surprised that none of them were rich. High prices had melted away their high wages.

And there was no "gravy" job waiting for Joe when he came back to General Motors. Instead of his old job assembling 250 window regulators an hour, he was made a bender operator.

His job now is to pick up an eight-foot-long piece of steel, slap it into the mold, push down the valve handle and then throw the whole thing back on the assembly line. He does that four and a half times a minute and if he misses a minute to tighten his belt, then he does nine the next minute.

"But that was okay with me," he added. "I didn't want to be a window regulator any more. It gets damn monotonous doing the same job day after day after day for so many years."

What Joe did object to, though, was getting ten cents less an hour on this job. Ten cents an hour means eighty cents a day, four dollars less a week. That would pay for most of his monthly gas and electric bill, or for the telephone or for the gasoline every week or for one-third of the interest on his insurance.

"One of the few dreams we've got left," said Joe, "is that some day, somehow, we'll save up enough money for a short trip to California, maybe even Mexico."

"And don't forget, Joe," said his wife, "we want to buy a house, too."

They were both quiet, thinking about that, and then Joe spoke, sounding bitter.

"Do you know how much money we've got saved up in the bank now?" he asked. He stretched out his words slowly. "We don't even have enough money to buy me a new suit. We just don't have a goddam."

There was silence again and then his wife tried to cheer up the conversation. "Thank God we're healthy," she said. Then, laughing, "We sure eat enough."

She explained that she just didn't believe in saving too much money on food because she knew you couldn't work well if you didn't eat enough. She knew that because while Joe was in the Army she got a job as an inspector at one of the Ford plants. Then, when she got laid off, she started working for a printing concern making up bags for fertilizer, but that's only seasonal work and she wouldn't be going back for a few more months.

As for Joe not getting any new clothes, they were so awful expensive and hard to get, she said. The only thing Joe had bought new was four pairs of underwear and it cost them seven dollars; before the war it was three pairs for only a dollar, the same stuff. That's why when Joe came out of the prison camp forty pounds lighter, she decided that instead of getting him new clothes, she'd just fatten him up until the old clothes fit. And she did. But now she's wondering whether that was such a smart idea after all, food prices being so high.

Why, eggs cost her fifty-nine cents a dozen from the farmer and at least ten cents more than that in the grocery, and before the war they were only thirty-nine cents. Even tuna fish used to cost her thirty-five cents a can and today she pays forty-six cents.

Maybe we spend a lot of money on food, she explained, but we save money on other things.

Joe, who had been listening glumly, now broke in:

"Yeah," he said, "we don't go to the movies at all now. It's lucky we don't care too much for the movies, isn't it, honey?"

She just nodded, but looked wistful.

"Another thing," said Joe, "what I can't understand is how some of my friends manage to raise children on the money they're making. Can you, honey?" he said, turning to his wife. She just nodded again.

Joe went on to say that General Motors still hadn't answered the union argument that they could grant the 30 per cent wage increase out of their old and new profits and still make more money than they ever made before. Even the latest Department of Commerce report agreed on that, said Joe. And it seemed logical to him that if the auto companies all gave a wage increase, more workers would have more money to buy cars.

"There's one big hitch," he said. "Even if the company does give me twelve bucks more a week, it won't mean a damn thing if they take the ceiling off of prices, because then we'll only pay more money for food and sure as hell they'll raise the rent and we'll be just as bad off as we are now.

"But on the other hand," he continued, "if we don't get that wage increase and they take the ceiling off of prices anyway, then I really don't know what the hell we'll do. I honestly don't. Do you, honey?" he said, turning to her again.

She was quiet for a minute, pursing her lips. "No, Joe," she answered slowly, "I just don't know where we can start economizing. We can't find any place cheaper to live and still live decent. Of course, there's the telephone we can get rid of, but that won't help much, and besides I think I'd rather eat less than give that up."

"There's the car," said Joe. "I can always sell that, except I won't get much, and besides, it's like selling part of the family."

His wife tried to smile. "The only thing I can think of, Joe," she said, "is that we put the lights out a little earlier at night."

Another train was going somewhere in a hurry and the house trembled again and the train noise faded away slowly.

Then it was in a strained hard voice that Joe said, "Now get this straight. I don't want to go out on strike. I'm not going to make any money while I'm striking. But if the company won't give us any more money, then the strike is the only weapon we've got left to use.

"I'm not asking for the moon," said Joe. "I just want to make a decent living."

"After all, we didn't have a damn thing to do with the taking of Paris. We just came in a couple days later when somebody got the bright idea of having a parade and we just happened to be there and that's all there was to it. It wasn't right that we should get the credit, but what can you do—that's just the way it goes. After all, we didn't get credit for a lot of things we did do," said Pfc. Verner Odegard, of Gonvick, Minnesota, a rifleman, of Company B, 1st Battalion, 19th Regiment, 28th Division.

"Getting back to Paris, as long as I live I don't guess I'll ever see a parade like that. Most of us slept in pup tents in the Bois de Boulogne the night before and it rained like hell and we were pretty dirty, so they picked out the cleanest guys to stand up front and on the outside. I had a bright new shiny patch, so they put me on the outside. It was a good place to be, too, because every guy marching on the outside had at least one girl on his arm kissing him and hugging him and marching right alongside of him.

"We were marching twenty-four abreast right down the Champs Elysées and we had a helluva time trying to march because the whole street was jammed with people laughing and yelling and crying and singing. They were throwing flowers at us and bringing up bottles of wine.

"The first regiment never did get through. The crowd just gobbled them up. They just broke in and grabbed the guys and lifted some of them on their shoulders and carried them into cafés and bars and their homes and wouldn't let them go. I hear it was a helluva job trying to round them all up later."

16

CASABLANCA TO COULTERVILLE

Young Ray Clutts stood outside his small wooden house, cracked his big mule whip and laughed. "Happy? Sure I'm happy. I'm home, ain't I?"

Home is Coulterville, Illinois, a coal-mining town, population 1,284. If you want to eat out, you go to Lydia's Café where you still get a real roast-beef lunch and homemade pie for forty cents. And if you want anything from garters to gossip, you go to the town crossroads, Tillie Robb's Variety Store. For the last word you go to white-haired Doc Hendrickson, who talks about his babies who are now veterans: "A few have gone to the big cities to try to make more money, but most of my boys seem to like it around here."

"There's something here that's different, though," said big-shouldered Merl Holmes, his eyes still rimmed with the black of the coal mines. "Don't know what it is, exactly. Seems like people don't neighbor as much as they used to, maybe. Lots more folks here have cars and they don't think nothing of driving sixty miles to St. Louis to see a show. But when it comes to walkin' across the street for some sociable talk, it seems to take 'em such a long time to get around to doin' it. Used to be a time when I could walk downtown and know just about everybody," Merl said sadly. "But no more."

Still, it had never occurred to him to leave Coulterville. All his roots were here. He was born and raised in this town and so was his wife and so were his folks and her folks and all their friends. For three years and twenty-one days in the Army, Coulterville had been his big dream. It was his way of life.

About working in the mine, sure it was dirty, maybe dangerous—"a guy got covered up today"—but even then it all depended on the way you looked at it. He met a cowboy out West once who said he would never have the guts to go down into a mine and Merl had laughed and said he felt the same way about getting on a horse.

Besides, everything was so different now that they had won their strike. Not that they like John L. Lewis. In Coulterville they belong to Local 61 of the Progressive Mine Workers. But there was no getting away from it: Lewis' strike demands were all okay. After all, if a worker gets crippled on the job, why shouldn't the company and the union chip in to support him?

"The point is, we coal miners don't expect to be as rich as Rockefeller or as poor as Job's turkey. All we want is a comfortable place to live and the chance to do an honest day's work for a decent living wage. And that's what we finally got here."

Merl's old job was to reinforce the old timbers down in the mine, but they won't let him do that any more. They gave him an easier job.

Merl opened his shirt, showing the long ugly scar on the side of his chest. "H-hour, D-day, Easy Red Beach," he said. "They had me blowing up obstacles. I still got some shrapnel inside."

Of the town's 132 servicemen, 11 didn't come back. Of the others, the Hortwich boy north of town who was going to open up a radio shop lost a leg, as did Stan Shaw, who still insisted on working the farm. There were others.

Biggest vet organization in town is the Veterans of Foreign

Wars, of which Merl is post commander. Twice a month the boys get together. Sandwiches, soft drinks, maybe beer, and lots of talk.

But now the war talk has a gloss to it. The mud and fear and stink have been pushed down deep inside themselves and the talk is mostly about the oo-la-la French girls and the whiteness of Casablanca and that furlough in Rome.

There's also a new tinge to their talk.

"If those newspapers and politicians want another war, let them do the fighting this time. . . ."

Other things, too. A roundhouse of curses against congressmen who killed the OPA; some general bitching about the housing situation; impatience with the loose, stupid mocking of the United Nations.

"Come on over and meet Ward Meyers," said Merl. "He chucks the coal and I weigh it."

Ward was pulling weeds out of his strawberry patch. A tall thin man with glasses, a former 36th Division rifleman who looked like a teacher.

"I used to have my own grocery for eight years, but I'm a darn sight happier in the mine," he said.

The thing he liked best was the seven-hour day—the chance to see some sunshine and play with his kid in the yard before he goes to bed.

"Bet you thought that coal miners were all hunch-backed and dirty and didn't know how to speak English," Ward smiled. "Most city folks think that. They're so surprised when they move around here and find that we live in nice clean houses and try to send our kids to college. We've got some college kids working in the mine right now. And why not? Fifty dollars a week out here means ninety in St. Louis."

"St. Louis? It's a nice place to visit if you want to see a ball game. But that's all."

He didn't like cities, didn't like traveling. What he wanted, he had.

"Come to think of it, mister, there is one more thing I want in my lifetime. Only one thing. No more wars. . . ."

On the front page of the Grenoble newspaper, there was this:
"Welcome!

"Yesterday, without warning, we saw them suddenly rising up at the far end of the Cours Jean Jaures. . . .

"At first no one dared to believe it. The Americans? They are here? Already? They are here? At last, astride their funny little jeeps, perched high on their heels, reminding one of the Far West, piloting their General Sherman tanks, henceforth so well known along the Route Napoleon.

"The crowd massed all along this fine avenue, just as it used to in the good old days of the Tour de France. What a glorious Tour de France this is. . . .

"Welcome to you all! You who have come from the distant provinces of Illinois, Ohio, Alabama or Texas. . . . Welcome to the citizens of New York and San Francisco, to all of you who have come to help France get rid of a nightmare which has lasted four interminable years, and to aid her to rediscover her true soul.

"Welcome to Grenoble, our town. Welcome to the Dauphine, our province."

17

BUNDLES FROM BRITAIN

SEVERAL dozen photographers were clustered around two cute brides in the "Argentina's" lounge, twisting for different angles, popping flashbulbs, yelling directions: "Turn this way, willya, babe? . . . How about a snappy smile? . . . A little more leg, please, that's it. . . ."

In the center of the room, huge klieg lights were brightly blazing on a play crib where three babies were bawling while a photographer furiously jiggled a doll and made funny faces and gurgling noises. One baby stopped crying for a minute to stare at him, then started all over again.

Near an exit, a newsreel man was prompting nine-year-old Donald Woods, who was dressed up in a cut-down soldier suit, all ready to invade Brooklyn. "Now, when I yell," explained the photographer, "you come running out on deck toward the rail, and, remember, try to look like you're sick."

All the others of the 200 members of the press were swarming down the lower decks, rushing in and out of the cabins where most of the 458 brides and their 175 children were waiting patiently. Some weren't so patient, though.

When one cameraman stuck his Speed Graphic too close to a woman's face, she snapped out, "What do you want, a photograph or an X-ray?" Another handed her baby to a friend and said angrily, "I'm going to go to the ladies' room and lock myself in and get away from this madhouse."

"Oh, damn," whimpered Ethel Mansfield, of Gloucester, England. "Why are they keeping us here? I want to get off this ship. I want to see my husband."

Mrs. Mansfield was worried about something else, too. She was going to Chicago, she said, and she didn't believe everything she heard about the gangsters there, but wasn't that the place where they recently found that little baby with its head cut off?

In the narrow passageway, a dark-haired pretty girl was telling a reporter, "The first thing my husband and I are going to do is to head straight for Florida where we can sort of relax and warm up."

Bubbling over in the next cabin, Mary Klein kept repeating, "I just can't believe I'm here. Really, I can't." She had been chopping down trees for the Women's Land Army and that's where she had met her Monroe. She only had one question: "Tell me," she asked, "is the Bronx really the most beautiful county in the United States, like Monroe says?"

A lieutenant colonel barged in and briskly asked if the women had any complaints or suggestions. They certainly had. There weren't enough disposable diapers and all the babies had diarrhea because their formulas weren't changed and the cribs weren't fastened down, so they rolled all over the cabin during that three-day storm. The colonel scribbled down everything in his notebook, smiled weakly and quickly back-tracked out of the room.

"What a trip," somebody moaned, "nothing to do but eat and sleep."

"And dream," said Linda Perfetti slowly. "It's been six months since I heard my man speak. It'll be strange listening to his funny accent again. He'll grab me and kiss me, and then he'll say, 'Who's your bloke' and then he'll kiss me again. And it'll be wonderful."

Then Mrs. Perfetti told how her husband used to be a professional boxer but now worked for a carpet mill in Amsterdam, New York. "He kept writing me that he was going to get me a washing machine, a rocking chair and a mirror, so that if I didn't take in washing for a living I'd be able to sit in the chair and look in the mirror and watch myself starve to death." She laughed hysterically. "Isn't he a scream?"

Interrupting the laughter was a young photographer with a press pass stuck in his hat. Very quickly, he rattled off a list of ten cities, ending up with Columbus, Ohio, and Brooklyn, New York.

"I'm from Columbus," one woman squealed excitedly as if she had won a sweepstakes ticket. Within seconds, he was popping pictures and the baby was bawling and the photographer was saying, "Kitchy-kitchy-koo" and "Wonderful . . . Wonderful. . . ."

One bystander whispered loudly how nice it would be if the man took pictures of all of them with their babies. She nudged a younger girl to go ask him but the girl shook her head vigorously and began to giggle.

The Columbus woman was telling the cameraman that her name was Dorothy Pfefferte and that her husband was a sailor. His ship wasn't coming in for a few days yet, so she planned to go shopping like mad before meeting his ship. "My husband married his landlady's daughter," she said, laughing.

There was a whirring static noise of the loudspeaker followed by a booming voice saying, "Your attention, please. . . ." and then a list of those women leaving in the first group.

"My husband won't be waiting for me anyway," explained a small, pale woman who was heading for Columbia, South Carolina. "My husband has been in the hospital for thirteen months now and I'm not sure when he'll get out. And when he does, he'll walk with a limp." Her face tightened. "But I don't care," she continued. "He's alive and I'm here and that's all that matters."

"I wonder how we're going to like it here," broke in a woman who said she was Evelyn Payne. She told about the daily orientation talks and the questions they had asked: why we drove on the wrong side of the street; what the relation was between prices and wages; were the American women really going to boo them when they walked off the ship; and did everybody truly think that they had funny accents?

"But it's not those things I'm worried about," said Mrs. Payne. "I'm worried about moving from a tiny town called Burton Latimer in Northamptonshire to a big city like Dallas, Texas. You see, I've never liked big cities. But I'll get used to it, won't I?"

On another bunk, a young mother was telling a well-dressed woman reporter how, at two-thirty that morning, the loudspeaker had broadcast, "Come on, girls. Get out of bed. It's the Statue of Liberty."

. "And the way we ran," she said. "The way we wrapped ourselves in blankets and raced on deck and there she was all lit up and we were so excited that nobody could say anything except one girl who kept screeching, 'We're here . . . we're here.' Then we all started singing 'God Bless America' and some of the girls began to cry and it was just like in the movies."

Up in the dispensary, Sergeant Joe Sharimataro told how this was the worst trip he ever had. "Those women almost drove me nuts," he observed. "This crib was too big and that one was too small and they all wanted diapers. Believe me, I almost went Section 8."

Then he relaxed and smiled. "But the kids were okay," he

reported. "I like kids. There was one cute one, about a year old, named Christobel, and I used to go up and play with her every day. Honestly, she didn't want to go back to her mother." He beamed. "Kids really go for me."

On the promenade deck there was a big bulletin board with a list of all who were going ashore in the first and second groups. Women were crowded around it, squeezed together. One finally pushed her way out. She was almost crying. "My name's not on it," she wailed.

"I just couldn't sleep last night," said Stuart Palmer, of Milford, Connecticut, who was standing in the hallway at the Red Cross Chapter House on Lexington Avenue. "I walked the streets until I was tired and then I stretched out on the bed and kept smoking one cigarette after another. I must have worn out the face of the clock looking at it so much."

He held up a small box. "Three pairs of nylons," he explained. "And I'll bet she doesn't even know what nylons are."

Standing next to him, Al Finnessey said that he had figured it out and it had cost him and his wife ninety dollars in special-delivery air-mail stamps since he left her in June. "We've been writing every single day," he said.

The cigarette almost burned his fingers and he dropped it and stepped on it. "Why didn't they let us meet them at the pier? It would have been so much easier. Gosh, I'm more nervous now than the day we got married."

A bus pulled up outside and the brides jumped out, looking around nervously. There were soon a dozen clinches and men were walking around with rouge on their lips and dazed eyes. One man leaning out of the balcony spotted his wife and yelled, "Jean . . . I'm up here, Jean . . . up here. . . ."

She looked up, waved hysterically, then stood there for a second just staring at him before she raced into the building.

Finnessey was still alone. "I guess she'll be in the next bus," he said.

Upstairs everything was confusion, with people talking and kissing and crying. One woman with a white tag that read "Counts, Gloria," was waiting for her husband to come back with her baggage. She was telling how disappointed she was with New York because it looked so much like London, when her husband appeared with the suitcases. He was all out of breath. "Come on, honey," he said, grabbing her. "Let's get out of here. We've got things to do."

The mine sweeper is in front of the whole war. For the dog-faces walking not too close behind him, slowly, the mine sweeper is one of the world's wonderful people. The mine sweeper walking with a dragged, heavy step, his shoulders hunched, his eyes staring at the ground, his arms slowly moving the vacuum-cleaner contraption from side to side.

And when he hears the loud buzzing, he stops. And when he stops, the whole war waits a minute. First he double-checks the buzzing. Then he sits down and stares at the ground as if he were watching an ant fight. Finally he pokes a little with something sharp and then he digs with his hands, gently, very gently.

But usually in war, the dogface is his own mine detector. A guy on patrol can't take a mine sweeper with him. He takes his chances, strains his eyes looking at snow, grass, horse dung, looking for three prongs or disturbed earth. Because underneath the ground somewhere may be powdered picric acid waiting to get excited. Foot pressure in the wrong place and a complicated human being becomes hamburger steak.

18

RETURN OF A HERO

WHEN he passed by Bub Wolfe's drug store, a man spotted him and came walking over fast, his face wide open in a smile, his hand outstretched. "Sure glad to see you again, Ben," he said. "We been reading about you in the newspapers and magazines and been hearing you on the radio. We folks are sure proud of you, Ben."

The words were warm and friendly but they made him feel awkward. He wanted to say something clever or else start laughing to change the subject, but instead he heard himself saying, "I just did my job."

That happened all day long, people stopping him on the street, pumping his hand, slapping his back, smiling at him, telling him what a big hero he was and how he really had put Hershey, Nebraska, on the map. Then there were the kids. Wherever he went, they stopped whatever they were doing to stare at him, counting aloud all his ribbons and battle stars and arguing among themselves which was the Distinguished Flying Cross and which was the Pacific Theatre ribbon. One kid walked up to him and shyly asked, "Are you really Ben Kuroki?" When Ben smiled and said yes, the kid's mouth just fell open and all he could say was, "Gee. . . ."

This was his home town, these were his neighbors. Most

of the memories of his twenty-seven years were tied up with them. This man had got him his first permit to trap beaver, that woman was one of his classmates, this little girl was the daughter of his best friend, that man used to work on their farm. He knew them all. Never had there been a single instance, a single word to let him know that his skin was yellow and theirs white.

Until Pearl Harbor Day. He had gone to that pool hall across the street to pick up a case of beer and some farmer had looked straight at him and said in a loud voice, "Well, I guess the Japs in this town are really celebrating tonight."

How sharply they still stuck in his mind: the words, the man, the room. And he remembered how he had seemed to freeze, sort of a physical-mental paralysis. He couldn't move, couldn't say anything, couldn't even think. Everything was just a big white blot. Then, somehow, he was walking in the street, walking quickly without knowing where, filled with a hot rush of anger, thinking of the million things he could have said and done. Why hadn't he socked the guy? Why didn't he tell everybody that he and his brother Fred already had decided to enlist in the Army the next morning?

That was four years ago, and yet it still hurt to think of it, even though it was such a small slap compared to all the things that had happened to him in the Army:

"Are you Chinese? No? Filipino? No? What? A Jap? Then what the hell are you doing in the American Army? We don't need your kind."

But everything was all right now. He had proved himself. And this was Hershey, his home. These were his friends. In Hershey, he knew that people were judged as individuals, not by who their father was, or the color of their skin, or the church they prayed in.

This was his Hershey, a tiny hunk of American democracy

sitting on both sides of U. S. Highway 30, only thirteen miles from North Platte, but you have to slow down or you might miss it. This was Hershey—sugar beets, corn, potatoes, cattle and 487 people. And when farmer Ben Lind hurt his leg and couldn't shuck his corn, somebody spread the news on the party line. That afternoon, Lind's farm was filled with neighbors shucking his corn, neighbors with all kinds of accents—Swedish, German, Italian, Irish, Japanese. But they were all friends and neighbors, all Americans. And when the federal government clamped down on the bank accounts of Japanese Americans, the Kurokis had a sudden rush of neighbors dropping in to offer what help they could.

These memories kept him going when the Army repeatedly turned down his requests for combat; when he found himself doing KP four times as often as anybody else; when he stopped taking passes to town because there was always some drunk who spotted him and started yelling; when he discovered that an F.B.I. agent was trailing him all the time, even after he had been checked and double-checked; and when he cried himself to sleep because he was so lonely for somebody to talk to.

Thinking of these things, Ben found himself automatically walking toward the school. It looked the same, except maybe a little smaller. Across the street the cows were still mooing and chewing in the field next to the church.

Soon he was inside, walking into the auditorium, hunting up his old desk to look for some scratched initials. All that fun that he, Bill Diamond, and Gordy Jorgenson used to have in this room, throwing spitballs and secretly chewing tobacco. And that class play they were all in. He was a French butler with a mustache and a goatee that kept falling off, Bill Diamond was dressed up like a girl, and Gordy had the leading role because he was the handsomest. Gordy was dead now.

There was his graduation picture, the whole class of fourteen students. How dressed-up and serious he looked. He must have known that the best fun was finished.

When Ben turned around, there was a thin, tall, graying teacher quickly coming over to introduce herself. "You must be Ben Kuroki," she said. "You don't know me, but of course I know all about you. I taught most of your younger brothers and sisters. Are you going to see the principal now?"

The new principal was a solidly built, serious young man who soon explained that he also taught several subjects as well as being athletic coach and the owner of a grocery store. He had talked to a lot of students and he knew how much they admired Ben, so would Ben please tell them some of his experiences? He could fill the auditorium in five minutes. Ben smiled, nodded. "Okay," he said.

He looked at their faces. Their ages ranged from the small, grade-school kids to the fuzzy-faced adolescents to the slightly swaggering seniors. War to them was still heroic and romantic like in the movies. What should he tell them?

First he told them what he knew they wanted to hear. He told them about some of the raids he was on: Bizerte, Naples, Messina, Rome, Wilhelmshaven, Ploesti. He told what thick flak looked like and how some of it once tore through his plane's tail and almost killed him; how he saw planes explode in mid-air, disappearing completely; what it was like in that night raid over Tokyo when his B-29 was bathed in searchlights for five full minutes; how it felt to sweat out every day's raid, coming back to stare at an empty bunk that last night belonged to a buddy who was alive.

He told about all the red tape he had to cut, that he had to get special permission from the Secretary of War himself before he could become a tail gunner. Then when he told why he tried so hard to get into combat, his voice was low, full of feeling, as if he were giving out his deepest secret.

It was because there were different kinds of Americans in his Liberator crew—Jewish, Polish, German, Italian, and even a full-blooded Indian. That, to him, was Democracy with a capital *D*. He was fighting for that.

Out in the street again, Ben walked with a light step, lazily thinking that maybe he'd go home and wander around the farm. He wondered if there was still a hole in that irrigation ditch where he used to go swimming until four in the morning sometimes.

He was passing the pool room when an old neighbor said hello and started asking him friendly questions about how he felt being home and what his plans were. Then the old man whispered, "Say, Ben, you can tell me this. Is it really true that the other Japanese farmer near you had a short-wave radio set and used to send messages to Japan?"

Ben started to laugh and then he suddenly realized that this man was serious. He didn't know what to say. The man was waiting for an answer. Finally, his words came slowly, "I hardly think so," he said.

When he walked away, he kept trying to rearrange the whole conversation in his mind. It was just one of those things, he told himself. Rumors like that will start anywhere, even in Hershey. But it didn't mean anything here. Hell, he knew these people.

Later that afternoon he heard something else. His land-lord and a gas-station attendant almost got into a fist fight because his landlord had said that Japanese American tenants were just as reliable as any white tenant he ever had. Ben triple-checked; it was true. But that gas attendant had always seemed like such a good guy, always kidded with him. It didn't make sense.

He was disturbed now, but he felt better when he dropped in at Bub Wolfe's place. Bub was always cracking jokes and this time a whole bunch of Ben's old buddies were there. They had all grown up together from hide-and-go-seek to basketball to war.

"Why don't you come down to the Legion meeting with us now?" said Gordy's younger brother, Virge. "All the boys you know will be there. Plenty of beer, too."

Sure, he'd go, he said. He planned to join several veterans organizations before he made up his mind which was his.

The Legion hall was on the top floor of a two-story building. It was a big room that badly needed cleaning. Next to the door was a small, pot-bellied stove, already getting red from too much heat. In back of the desk was a huge American flag and on the wall right next to it was a rifle complete with bayonet, World War I style. In the center of the room were three full cases of beer.

Sitting behind the desk was the post commander, young enough to be the son of either of the two men who flanked him. "The old Legionnaires gave him the job just to prove that they really intend to hand over the Legion to us World War II veterans," said Virge. "Those old boys deserve a lot of credit for keeping the Legion going until we got back. It almost died out a lot of times."

On the post commander's left was a big, heavy man, the only one in the room wearing a Legion cap. On his right was a thin man with a small face. The other older men sat next to each other in small clusters, most of them tired-looking farmers, not talking much.

When the room was almost full, the thin man whispered something to the post commander, who then loudly called the meeting to order. The big, heavy man started reading the roll call. Most of the names called weren't present. Virge explained it, "They're still in the Army. Their folks and friends signed up for them. Some of them won't even know they're in the Legion until they get back."

Next on the agenda was the treasurer's report. He was the thin man behind the desk telling that they paid so much for the band and so much for that damn government tax and that left them only twenty dollars net profit on the last dance they had. While he was talking, four older men came in, walking a little unsteadily, greeting all their friends in too-loud voices. The older members smiled nervously.

The trio behind the desk held a quick powwow and decided it was time to induct the new members. The post commander finally persuaded one of the older men to act as sergeant-at-arms and somebody else got the Legion flag, which was embroidered with "Paul R. Martin Post 279." Then the acting sergeant coughed and said, "You boys fall in here."

Being one of the few still in uniform, Ben felt awkward. But then, so did the others. They shuffled around slowly, looking sheepishly at each other. The commander very quickly read the Legion laws and oath. It was too fast for Ben to absorb all of it but he caught such phrases as "justice and equality," "democracy for all," and "without prejudice of race, color or creed."

It was done. He was a member. The commander was shaking hands with each of them and the treasurer was collecting the two-dollar initiation fee and selling Legion emblems.

Most of the recruits bought them. Then the almost-forgotten sergeant barked out with, "Okay, boys, you can sit down now."

After the short ceremony, the treasurer broke the silence by whispering with embarrassing loudness to the post commander, "Go ahead, tell them about getting new members. Go ahead, tell them."

The commander seemed ready to say something to the treasurer, looked around and thought better of it. He went into a snappy sales talk on how every new member ought to pledge himself to get another member so that they could really build up the post.

That seemed to satisfy the treasurer, who then brought up the subject of how to get more money into the treasury. Since the dance didn't do it, he suggested they ought to have a barbecue with an attached gambling concession. There was a man in North Platte who would guarantee them either a percentage of the profits or a flat guarantee if they let him take charge of the gambling setup. Another Legion Post did the same thing and made a profit of nineteen thousand dollars. He himself didn't believe it until he met a farmer friend of his who personally admitted that he had lost fifteen hundred dollars there in one night. The last he heard was that the firemen in town were thinking of doing the same thing, so he suggested that they beat them to the punch. A committee should be formed right away to get all the details, he said. After a quick vote, the committee was chosen.

That done, the commander mentioned the matter of getting a memorial plaque in honor of their war dead. He read different descriptions from a fancy folder, giving each price.

"They're pretty expensive," said the treasurer. "I'll bet some goddam Jew owns all those companies. They own everything else in this country."

A man near Ben chimed in, "Yeah, those Jews can't think of anything else but making money." There was some more of the same.

Ben froze. He wanted to ask them if they had forgotten so quickly the words in that Legion oath, the ones about equality and democracy. He wanted to plead with them to remember that if they let intolerance sneak inside of them now they would never again be able to treat people as individuals, but as colors and religion and creeds. Then there would be no more of that wonderful democracy in Hershey.

He wanted to say, "Don't make me feel that I fought for nothing."

But he said nothing. His tongue was paralyzed, like so many times before when people had called him names. And soon it was too late. The meeting was over. The men were grabbing bottles of beer and somebody was yelling at him over the noise of the crowd, "Say, Ben, you wanna play a little poker?"

The street was dark and empty and cold and he suddenly felt lonely. In the car, driving home, he remembered something the principal had told him after his speech:

"Now, Ben, wouldn't it be wonderful if the boys coming home could really practice the kind of democracy they were supposed to have fought for?"

He was a mealy-mouthed runty guy, and he hit the floor every few minutes, every time the doughfoot hit him. The dough would pick him up, sock him a few times, and let him fall, then pick him up and do it all over again. The runty guy was a scientist who helped invent the V-bombs.

They found him in a huge underground factory setup at Nordhausen with a half-dozen corridors a kilometer long, sliced by several dozen other corridors—all air-conditioned and lit by phosphorescent light. Some of the V-bombs were still in the assembling stage.

. . . Those hundreds of kids back in London lined up around the building with their mothers, waiting to get into the store because they were selling ice cream again after so many years and some kids had never had any ice cream before. And then the V-2 coming out of the soundlessness of nowhere, blasting kids into pieces for blocks around. . . .

The photographer said to the doughfoot, "Would you please lift that runt up again once more and sock him again so I can get a picture of it?"

"The pleasure's all mine," said the soldier.

19

TOWN OF TOMORROW

This was the perfectly planned town of Richland, fifteen thousand people living in one of the three homes of American atomic energy—no slums, no crime, no poor, no shortages. Everything reborn brand-new off an architect's drawing board. The town of tomorrow.

Lester Fishback sat at the small table in the dimly-lit basement bar, staring gloomily at his half-empty glass of beer. He was a slow-talking man in his middle thirties and he wasn't very happy, he said. What's more, he knew a lot of other people who weren't. Two hundred and forty-seven people, to be exact.

That was the total population of the old Richland, a tiny town, miles from the main road, tucked in between the Columbia and Yakima rivers. A tiny town with a good irrigation setup and a healthy bank balance. Blacksmith shop, general store, pool hall, druggist. There was a weekly dance at the Grange Hall and everybody went. If a farmer got sick, his neighbors took in his crop. The town took care of its own.

"Just a small sleepy little place," continued Lester, "only we never thought of it that way. I had ten acres of good rich land. My family always had plenty to eat—"

His voice broke off and you could hear the noise of the

[163]

juke box and the slot machine and the laughter of the people at the next table.

Lester killed his beer, then gripped the empty glass with both hands as if he were squeezing it. His words came out sharp, bitter:

"This country's so big. There are so many thousands of acres nobody lives on. Why did they have to tear up my town?"

But this new Richland had everything: huge supermarkets, brand-new homes for cheap rent, beautiful new post office, big bowling alleys, wide clean streets, modern movie houses. And wasn't he making a good salary?

He hit the table with his hand, the glass still in it. "I never worked for wages in my whole life. I don't like working in a factory. I like my own piece of ground where I'm my own boss, where I can do anything I want to. I like to grow things. . . ."

His words were coming out more quickly now. The thing that hurt him most when he came home from the Pacific was when he got off the bus. He didn't know where he was. It was just completely different. Everything. He was so lost, he had to ask an MP to help him find his old farm. Then when he got there, he was sorry he had come. The grapes and asparagus were all dried up just as if somebody had walked off and left them, and there was this huge power line over the place where the house was. All of it dry and dead.

But it had to be done. Didn't he say he was in the Pacific? If it wasn't for the atomic bomb, he might be dead somewhere in Japan right now. Wasn't that true?

"Yeah," he said, nodding his head slowly. "I guess that's true."

Besides, if he didn't like working here in a factory, why didn't he leave this town and buy some land somewhere. After all, this was a free country.

He stopped nodding and his voice got sharp again. "Did you ever hear of the word money? Don't worry, when we make enough, we'll get out of here and buy some more land. I'm not sentimental about this town any more. This isn't my Richland. I don't even know if I want to be buried here."

Diagonally across the room, closer to the bar, young pretty Helen Boling laughed at your question. Her laugh was loud, almost slightly hysterical. There were several empty beer glasses on the table.

"The old Richland? Mister, that was really what you call a dead town, but really dead. Absolutely." She laughed again. "The smartest thing I ever did was to get out of here and go to New York. Now there's what you call a real town. Why did I come back?" She winked at her friend and they both laughed. "Oh, I had my reasons."

Her laughter and the blaring of the juke box were cut out completely when you closed the door behind you upstairs. The building was the only large old building still standing in town. It used to be the schoolhouse but the Legion had taken it over and redecorated it. George Speight, a thin, anxious-looking man, had his office on the main floor. He was the local representative of the Veterans Administration.

Yes, he was here when they first started building the $350,000,000 plutonium plant. It was the biggest trailer camp in the world then; eighty thousand workers and they drank more beer than the whole city of Seattle. Probably made more money, too. A regular draft dodgers' paradise. You could walk around any day and recruit enough healthy guys to fill up a regiment.

"Hell, you can't blame the vets here for being bitter. Christ, how would you feel if you gave up the best years of your life and then came here to work for a guy who made twice as much money as you did, even though he wasn't any older or any smarter than you. Guys who came here to get out of the war and sit on their fannies in these lush jobs. You know what any vet thinks of those guys."

To change the subject, what about the atomic bomb? He was in contact with more veterans than anybody else, what did they think about it? How much had it changed their lives, their plans, their thoughts?

"Well, to be honest with you, most of the guys don't think much about it any more. At first they were all scared to talk about it on account of the security. Now they're just tired of talking about it. It's just another job. They're bored."

Bored? If the people of any town anywhere should feel deeply about the bomb, shouldn't they feel it here? Here, more than anywhere, the workers should have nightmares about it.

Not Emmett Elliott, though. Emmett was a fireman on the No. 2 truck.

"Number 2 only goes out on the big fires." He grinned. "Frankly, I haven't been on a fire yet. This town's so new and clean, there just aren't any fires."

That didn't bother him too much. He still liked his job. Drill twice a day, keep the truck clean and polished, practice first aid. He liked the other guys, too, the social life of the firemen's club, the uniform.

"It's a helluva lot better than sawing grass," said the young man from Moberly, Missouri. Still, he was also qualified as an electrical repair man, a diesel operator, a railroad construction worker. But he knew lots of skilled veterans who were doing unskilled jobs because they didn't have the seniority. But none of them could kick much; they were all getting higher wages than most skilled workers outside Richland.

"Now look at me, I'm happy. I almost couldn't be happier."

He had come here immediately after his army discharge because his wife was working here. Together they got a new Type A home with two bedrooms, three rooms downstairs, two rooms upstairs, all for forty-seven dollars a month. And he had fine, friendly neighbors, too.

Did they ever talk much about atomic energy?

"Not any more. But I'll tell you this. Everybody's sure a lot happier since we're converting to peacetime stuff. A lot of folks just didn't feel right about making bombs when there wasn't any war going on."

Sitting in the spectator seats, watching the bowling, the young man in the old combat jacket blurted out a quick answer to a pointed question:

"Confidentially, I'm getting the hell out of this town as soon as I can. They say it's a model city—well, it's too damn model for me."

To him, it was a small town with a small mind. He couldn't get over it: people working on the most important single thing in the world and most of them didn't know what the hell it was all about. Even worse, most of them didn't care. Just another job. Good money, cheap rent, stocked stores, comfortable homes. They couldn't see ahead of their noses, or they didn't want to see. He knew lots of guys who came here and got fed up and pulled out.

All you had to do was get drunk once in this town and get caught, he went on. The local Gestapo could barge into your house anytime without a warrant and if they smelled liquor on your breath and reported you, then you were fired. And if you were fired, you were evicted. Just like that.

But that didn't bother him so much. What bothered him most was the mentality of the town, so similar to the small town he came from and he thought it would be so different.

"Here's what I mean. Sure the bomb shortened the war

and saved my life, but someday soon it might kill me. The way the whole world seems to be sliding toward destruction and nobody seems to be doing anything about it. The people aren't getting excited. If they'd only get up and all yell about it to their politicians, then something would be done. And you'd think the yelling would start right here in Richland, where the whole thing was partly born. But I tell you, it's just as if they don't want to think about it, as if they're pushing it away from their minds. . . ."

His voice lowered. "Do you know another reason I want to get away from here?" Unconsciously he cracked his knuckles. "I'm scared," he said. "The whole thing scares the pants off me."

"Just before we pulled out, the CO read us this message from Eisenhower about how we were all crusaders and all that, and it made us all feel pretty good," said Sgt. Robert Miller, of the 502d Regiment, who was in the sixteenth plane over France.

"It seemed like a long trip, but it was only two hours. It was a long two hours though because it was so hot in the plane and with all that 120 pounds of stuff on us, most of the guys got a little sick.

"You don't talk much. I didn't say a damn word. And don't ask me what I was thinking about because I don't remember. I guess I was thinking a little about everything.

"And don't ask me what I saw when the chute opened, because I don't remember that either. But I remember everything after I hit the ground. Seeing a guy burning in the air. Things like that.

"The most terrible thing is when you hit the ground and you don't see anybody and you don't hear anything and you're all alone. Being lonely like that is the worst feeling in the world."

20

HOMELESS ON THE RANGE

The big bulging woman was laughing so hard, the tears formed mascara streaks down her cheeks. Still laughing, she leaned over, slapped the man on the back and said, "You sure know some hot ones, Jack."

Across from the bar were the ten noisily clicking slot machines, a large crowd of tense faces quietly watching the twirling pictures. Deeper inside the restaurant, a huge red-faced man grabbed an embarrassed waitress, trying to make her dance, at the same time loudly singing, "Roll me over . . . in the clover. . . ." Watching all this were three giggling girls and their three young boy friends, one of whom wore a big badge, "I MAY BE BALD, BUT I'M NOT TOO OLD."

Dick stood at the bar, listening to the laughter, envying the red-faced man and the young kids, suddenly wishing he were very, very drunk or very, very young. But you got drunk after a rodeo, not before. Horses sense things like that, especially those bucking horses. There was a blonde sitting alone in that corner booth, not bad. If he wasn't feeling so crummy right now, he might go over and make a play. But he wasn't in the mood for the routine of phony smiles and fast talk. Now if he was only a little tight. . . .

Outside, he walked down Evanston's Main Street, smiling

at the cop shepherding a happy drunk to a quiet corner. The cops would be busy tonight. All year long, the 3500 residents of this town waited just for this, their big fun; their one chance to break loose from the tied-down living of a small Wyoming cattle town. For one night, to lose themselves in the noise and excitement.

In the blocked-off side street, Dick saw the long wooden table where people crowded around playing bingo, a smaller table where they played blackjack standing up, then a hodge podge of tents where you hit dolls with baseballs and bought pennants and popcorn. It never changed, the same stuff every year. Even the small circular swing for the kids and the auction.

God, look what they were auctioning off to the kids—gas masks and cartridge belts. For kids. God Almighty. The last auction he remembered here, they were bidding for baseball bats.

The last auction he remembered here. . . .

Hotshot Dick McDaniels, the boy wonder . . . not even twenty-one and already had 1500 rodeo points for the national cowboy championship. Bulls, bareback, bucking horses, anything, he'd ride anything. Hotshot Dick McDaniels, there's a boy who's going places, yes siree.

Going places . . . yeah . . . the Siegfried Line.

Now what? Well, now he was almost twenty-six, an old cowboy with a busted hand. No more bareback riding for a while, no more bulls. Funny about those bulls. Before the war, bulls were so easy. Sure, they scared the hell out of him —ever since he saw one rip out a guy's guts—but, still, once he got on them, he stayed on. Now he wasn't scared any more, but they threw him every time. Funny.

If he had any brains, he'd get the hell out of this town, right now. He'd catch the next train, no matter where it went. Settle down and learn a trade and find him a good wife. That's what he should do. Quit all this crazy chasing around, one rodeo to another rodeo all year long. What kind of life was it anyway? Seventeen hundred cowboys in the Rodeo Cowboys Association and maybe half of them made expenses, if they were lucky. The other guys would just keep paying their entry fees and every once in a while, they'd win a hundred bucks, maybe. And if a bull ripped open a cowboy's belly or kicked him in the head, and he died, the RCA would bury him for free. That is, if his dues were paid up. What the hell kind of a life was that?

Oh, what was he blowing his top for? It wasn't going to make any difference. It never would.

The circular swing had stopped and some more kids piled on. Dick saw a cowboy lift his son and drop him gently into a seat. Those were the guys who had it really tough, the married ones with kids. This gypsy living wasn't for them. Kids needed to be in one place, a home, school. The wives didn't have it too easy either. Which one of the boys was it who sent his wife home to her mother because he wasn't making enough for the two of them to eat right?

Dick left the carnival street, walking quickly until the town was suddenly black and quiet, except for a glimmer from City Hall's back room. When Dick opened the door, his eyes blinked at the brightness but he could see the room was almost full. There was a short line of cowboys waiting to pay their fifteen-dollar entry fee.

He knew almost everybody there. Dammit, here it was just like every other entry room at every rodeo: the vets sitting by themselves in one part of the room, the non-vets bunched together on the other side. Nobody said why, nobody ever talked about it at all, but everybody knew. It was shame and bitterness. The shame of the non-vets who stayed home and made all the money in war jobs, the bitterness of the vets who never let themselves forget the time they had lost.

For him the dough didn't mean much. Anyway, it wasn't the big thing. The big thing was the four years spent away from horses. Four years without even seeing a horse, with nobody to talk to. That's what hurt most, nobody who understood how he felt. Those guys in the 65th Division were wonderful all right, real buddies, but they didn't understand. If he had ever told them that he missed horses as much as they missed their women—they would have razzed the hell out of him.

But it was true. Ever since he was a kid, ever since he got that first Shetland pony in the fifth grade. Then that beautiful Palamino, and the big bay horse. Ever since the first time he ever rode a bucking horse, the crazy mixed up feelings of nervous excitement just before he dropped down on the horse, then trying to stick, trying to outguess him, feeling like he always felt whenever he sang the "Star-Spangled Banner" real loud. How could he ever talk about it to anybody without sounding either queer or corny? Oh, why the hell didn't the Army put him in the cavalry when he enlisted?

Still, he couldn't kick. He was alive. He still had two arms and two legs. He almost didn't.

If he ever got married, he wanted a woman who loved horses like he did. He wanted a woman who wouldn't laugh if he told her that his biggest thrill in the whole damn war was the time the 65th captured a German cavalry unit and he picked himself out a horse. A beautiful big black sorrel. Rode so smooth. Didn't ever take much rein. The warmth and excitement that was in him the first time they went riding, the deep feeling he could never tell anybody about. They'd spent a whole month in that rest area, a whole month with that horse. It almost made up for four years.

[174]

After he paid his entry fee, Dick sat down next to Bill Whitney. Bill was telling a group of vets how he was in the Navy all the time, and how the ship's motions gave him plenty of practice for the bucking horse. Everybody laughed. Their talk then turned to pipe dreams: they all had the same one. Some day they were all gonna head East and try out Madison Square Garden for the big prize money. All of them had heard of the lucky cowboys who drew good horses out of the hat and made as much as six thousand dollars in one day. Well, that was their pipe dream: they'd win the six thousand and get a GI loan, too; then they'd buy a small ranch with some cattle, brood mares, and jackasses. You could always make money raising mules. Anyway, in the summer when the rodeos came around, they'd take time out to enter a few shows, just to keep their hand in, you understand.

Pipe dreams. Most of them would ride in third-rate shows for the rest of their lives, never even get up to Cheyenne or Pendleton. And when they got too old for the bucking horses, they'd go in for calf-roping, and when they got too old for that, they'd help the clowns or water the horses. Then they'd die, and the RCA would bury them, if their dues were paid up.

This entry room was like a mirror: the hotshot kids riding their first shows; the veterans filled with feelings of uncertainty, their best time behind them; the older cowboys living on yesterdays. Here was his past, present, future.

When he left them, they were still talking. God, tomorrow he had to win something. He had eaten up most of the dough he saved in the Army. The last prize money he won was back in Lehigh. He was hot that day, until he got thrown and kicked in the tail. That was two hundred bucks. It was gone already. So was the twenty-five bucks he picked up judging that show in Blackfoot. This damn busted hand. . . .

Back at the blocked-off street, he looked at some of the faces watching the bingo game. Faces on the fringe of the crowd—they were as lonely as he was.

He hesitated for a minute in front of the bar, then walked in.

"Everybody asks me what the Falaise Gap looked like and they look at me kinda funny when I tell them I don't know. All I know is that I was with Company D, 1st Battalion, 318th Regiment, 80th Division, and we were green as hell because this was our first big action. We were so green that we didn't even dig in. I remember they brought up these tanks and fired point-blank direct fire at us, and they got our battalion CO and the S-2 on the same day. We were up there five days and we lost a helluva lot of men. We were just green, that's all. And I never did get to see this Falaise Gap. There was just this small hill and a little town right next to it. I don't even remember the name of the town."

21

EPTHEMIOS

His name was Epthemios Papadopoulos, he said, but everybody called him Kelly. Even in the Army, they used to call him Kelly. Where the hell they got Kelly from, he didn't know.

He was a slim, dark young man with a big "W" on his sweater and he looked too young to be a bartender. The bar was one of those converted basements, once part of an old schoolhouse. The American Legion had spent three thousand dollars decorating it with wagon wheels, cowboy murals, dim lights, and slot machines. It was still early so there were only a half dozen people in the room, all of them crowded around the slot machines.

"You can ask anybody," said Epthemios, "this is the best club in Benton County. And if they'd let us sell beer every night instead of only twice a week, we'd clean up a fortune." He looked at the polished bar and smiled brightly, "Pretty good job for a punk kid of twenty-three, ain't it?"

Not only was he the bartender, he explained, but he was the manager of the whole clubhouse, had all the responsibility for the money, the ordering, and everything. "I even sweep up the place."

His face was serious now. "The way I look at it, you can always have your fun. But when a rainy day comes along, you don't want to be caught with your pants down. So when opportunity knocked on my door, I grabbed it."

He was gesturing with his right hand. Suddenly he stared at it, straightened it, and tried to hold it out steady, trying not to show the strain in his face. But his whole hand kept shaking visibly and finally he put it down quickly. He tried to smile. "It used to be a lot worse. This job's been good for me."

The Army had kept him in a hospital for a long time before they discharged him. Then he was okay for a while, until he started school. He'd get into a nervous sweat waiting for the teachers to call on him, trying to do his homework, wondering what good it was. Too much pressure built up inside of him and he got sick again. Finally, he quit.

"So there I was, free as a bird. But I didn't know what the hell to do with myself. That's when I got this bright idea."

The bright idea was to hitchhike around the country. Plan out a route with stop-offs at the different places his buddies lived, then start moving.

First stop, lower Manhattan.

"There was this buddy of mine who clerked in one of those big department stores. He fed me a line of bull about how he was learning the business from the ground up and how they promised him an important job in the advertising department. He was like that overseas, too. Always daydreaming, always talking big."

Next was McKeesport, Pennsylvania, where his friend was a grease monkey in a gas station.

"I couldn't get over it—the change in a guy. Whole personality was different. Like day and night. When that guy was my first sergeant he was the toughest guy you ever saw. Here he was just a grease monkey saying 'yessir' all the time. He didn't loosen up till we got drunk."

They all got drunk with him, filling themselves with warm, wonderful, dressed-up memories. But they all woke up with the same hangovers.

"Now take this babe in Chicago. She was a Wac I knew in London. One of the cutest little things on two feet. Stacked just right. Over there she wouldn't let anybody touch her because she was engaged. Me and her was like brother and sister. Well, you know what happened. The old story. Some other gal back here hooked her guy. When I saw her, she was crying in her beer. She coulda had a million guys over there, if she just crooked her little finger."

His girl? She was dead.

"I went to see her folks. They live in a little town in Iowa. Just an old couple on a small farm. They didn't have any other kids. When I came, they didn't know what to do with me. The old lady fed me so much stuff, I musta gained ten pounds that week. Yeah, I spent a week there. The old man needed help, see, so I just hung around. They wanted me to stay for keeps but can you picture me a farmer?"

Then there was this kid in Las Vegas who also tried to talk him into settling down.

"He was in my outfit and I always sorta took care of him. You know, I showed him the ropes, helped him out in a couple fights, put him to bed when he passed out. Y'see, I was older'n him. He was just a kid, only eighteen; I was nineteen.

"Know what? The kid's ma even hinted around that if I stayed there, she'd fix me up with a nice girl and maybe I'd fall in love and get married. Ain't that a hot one?"

Some of the slot machine losers came over for more beers. Epthemios had a clean, efficient way about him behind the bar and he knew how to kid his customers. When he came back, he was still smiling.

"Now where was I? Oh yeah, Las Vegas. Well, I mighta

stayed there, see, but I promised this buddy in L.A. that I'd come out and see him. He said he had some kind of hot deal cooking. Besides, I'd never been to California."

Well, what about the hot deal?

Epthemios screwed up his face and crossed his hands. "Phony. Strictly phony. I didn't want no part of it. I got out of there, but quick."

There were some other stops, but it was the same story. The same drinking, bitching, wistfulness.

"So finally I come up here to Washington. I gotta friend working up at the plant here and he told me about this job. Jobs like this don't grow on trees. Now I'm from the big city myself—Worcester, Mass.—but the way I see it, a big city is only good when you got a good job. Anyway, the way I feel now, maybe a small town's better for me.

"Besides, I was running short of dough and too much bumming around and drinking wasn't so good for me. Otherwise, I might've gone to Florida. I've always wanted to go down to Florida. Only trouble is, I don't have any buddies down there."

He looked toward the door. A few more customers were coming in. Epthemios went on talking. "And like I said, this town is good for me. I'm not so nervous like I used to be. So I guess I'll stick here for a while—"

He carefully examined his fingers.

"—until I get sick again. Then I'm pulling out. I can't stand it when people start feeling sorry for me."

The big brass of the 36th were all having headaches. They knew just how tough the Moselle crossing was going to be. The Germans were dug in ready and waiting. It would be a bloody business.

Somebody announced that the mayor of Roan-aux-Bois wanted to see them on urgent business. They must have cursed to themselves and said what the hell does he want, and somebody went to find out.

He was Monsieur Gribelin, retired French naval officer, sixty years old, if you please, and when they found out what he had to say, they almost kissed him. His was a gift of American lives.

There was a jeep-sized pass that led to a shallow part of the Moselle where the water was only waist deep and the current was slow and there was plenty of cover for vehicles. It was a short cut to Eloyes, where he went to see his daughter on Sundays. It would take them right behind the German positions.

It made a peculiar parade in the dark, cloudy night with the rain coming down in drizzles, the old man walking proudly with his face shining and his chest out, and the tired Joes and their jeeps trailing close behind.

22

GI CONGRESSMAN

S<small>HE</small> bounced by both secretaries, swished inside the Congressman's private office, waved a letter in her right hand, and loudly announced just who she was and what she wanted. She was a registered voter in the Democratic party, she said, and she wanted him to get her husband out of the Occupation Army in Germany and bring him back to her bed and board.

As for the letter, it was short and sharp. It said, "Honey, it sure looks like they're jerking us soldiers around over here in Europe. You better go down to Washington and get a hold of our congressman, whoever he is, and tell the big bum that we got a lot of votes in our family and he just won't get any of them in the next election unless he gets me out of this hole."

When Congressman William J. Green Jr. told this story, there was no smile in his voice. "Because it really isn't funny," he said. "These women keep coming into my office, crying their hearts out and showing me letters from their husbands and I know exactly how they all feel about it, especially how the guys feel."

Green knows, because only last year he was still a private first class, peeling potatoes in a quartermaster company kitchen in Camp Lee, Virginia. One of two GI's elected to the seventy-ninth Congress (the other is his Camp Lee buddy, Melvin

Price, of Illinois), Green represents the Fifth Congressional District, that northeast part of Philadelphia where they make everything from ships to silk stockings.

"But it's no cinch being a freshman congressman," said thirty-six-year-old Green, "because there's more red tape in one square foot of Congress than there is in the whole American Army, and I'm not kidding."

He told about the tight seniority system in committees, how a small clique of reactionary southern Democrats could say yes or no on whether vital bills ever even got on the floor of Congress. He told how new bills either got stuck on the first stop in some pigeonhole or else were copy-catted by a dozen different congressmen, without the change of a comma.

"A new guy just doesn't have a chance here," he said. "You come here all hepped up with shiny new ideas about what you're going to do to make a better America and you talk yourself hoarse in Congress and nobody seems to be paying too much attention. Then you start proposing bills and resolutions and you wait for things to happen, but nothing happens."

Green has averaged almost a bill a month, most of them concerning veterans and all of them still sleeping soundly in different committees. Among other things, Green asked that returning veterans be allowed to vote in the South without paying the poll tax, that the GI Bill be further liberalized, that all discharged soldiers get a civilian clothing allowance, that certain long distance calls from army camps be tax-exempt, that additional West Point and Annapolis cadets be selected from sons of fathers killed in this last war, that GI's be officially represented at any peace table.

GI's at the peace table also was the theme of Green's maiden speech in Congress last February. He had also stressed that qualified GI's should be placed in key posts in key government agencies "to give the veteran a voice in his own destiny, to see that the war has not been fought in vain."

That speech caused a lot of comment, brought in a lot of mail.

"It sort of makes us feel good that our own Billie Green has what it takes," wrote one voter. "We know that your interest in the serviceman is the biggest thing in your mind and heart. You can be sure that the news clipping will reach the South Pacific."

But, as usual, most of the letters were still from people who wanted something. There was the mother who recommended her son for a West Point appointment "because he's a perfectly marvelous boy and everybody likes him"; the guy who wanted the Congressman to bring his girl here from England so he could marry her; the man who had invented all kinds of wonderful inventions and would Green please take care of all the complicated details like patenting them; the soldier who wanted to get out of the Army because "I would much rather go to Lafayette College"; the father who wanted a thorough investigation of the whole War Department because his son had been court-martialed just because he went AWOL when they shipped his combat outfit overseas. "He came back after V-J Day," explained the father, who couldn't understand it; and then there was the prominent Philadelphia retailer who wrote:

Dear Congressman Green:
 The underwear situation here is bad. We need more underwear. See what you can do.

But even more depressing than the underwear situation was the Army-Navy football game.

"I got hundreds of letters and telephone calls from people who wanted free passes," said unsmiling Green. "You know

[187]

how it is. People all figure that what the hell, a congressman is a big shot, the least he can do is to get me a free ticket to a football game because didn't I vote for him?"

But Green only had sixteen passes, plus what he could scrounge from other congressmen. That still left him several hundred enemies. And even some of the lucky ones wrote him bitter notes because their seats were either in the temporary stands or at the five-yard line or behind some big post.

"You can't win," said Green sadly, "but what's more important, with all this running around for football tickets and underwear and things like that, I hardly have enough time to do the job I was elected to do."

That job includes such things as a long visit with General Bradley to discuss the possibility of getting a veterans' hospital located in Philadelphia. It also meant getting sandwiched in between the American Battle Monuments Commission and Prime Minister Attlee to talk to President Truman about demobilization speed-up. But more than anything else, it means his work on both the Veterans and Labor Committees where he's helped cause such explosions as the investigation of veterans' hospitals and the indictment of forty firms for monopolistic practices in making artificial limbs.

Sometimes both committees will hold equally important meetings at the same time and Green almost has to toss a coin. During one of those times, Chairman Rankin of the Veterans Committee took advantage of Green's absence to sneak through a sugar-coated bill designed to cripple unions without really helping any veterans.

The news got to Green quickly and the next morning he and ranting Rankin were tangling words. Green talked about how the cause of labor was all tied up with the cause of the veterans and that "we must not forget that manufacturers today are trying to break the back of labor and break unions while waving the flag in their hands.

"As for the gentleman from Mississippi," Green said, "if he's so anxious to help the veterans, why doesn't he support my bill to let veterans vote without paying the poll tax?"

That shut Rankin's mouth and it also caused a lot of congressmen to start calling Green "the GI watchdog."

Green's already-fat mailbag swelled even fatter after that. Veterans wrote in: "I guess you know better than the Rankins how the GI feels." "We'd like to see this Rankin tossed out on his ear. What a phony to have as head of the Veterans Committee." "We need more guys in Congress like you, Green."

All this was sweet music to Green, who has been part of politics ever since he voted for the first time (Roosevelt, 1932). He still says that the big thing that gave him the political itch was a burning speech somebody made to his graduating class at St. Joseph's College, saying how important it was for liberal, educated people to get into politics and kick out the racketeers and reactionaries.

For seven years after that, Green was the big boy in the Thirty-third Ward in Kensington, where he had lived all his life. From ward leader to district leader, almost to City Council (he lost by 1800 votes), he finally went to Governor Earle's personal staff, where he helped shape Pennsylvania's "little New Deal." During all this, he also got married and produced four children. But the draft still wanted him.

In the Army, though, Green wasn't coy about being a congressman. He wanted the job badly. But still he told his civilian friends one thing, "When you run my campaign, don't wave around my uniform to get votes. Don't post any pictures of me in uniform. If I get in, I want to get in on my own."

Soon after he was elected, he got a letter from a classmate of his at Ascencion Parochial School who was then with G Company, 337th Infantry, 85th Division, in Italy:

"When a friend of mine asked if I knew a Bill Green from G Street in Philadelphia I said, 'Yeah, why?' And when he showed me the story in *Yank* about you being a GI congressman, you could have knocked me over with a feather. I'm sure glad that somebody from my old neighborhood made the news."

In the same mailbag was a short letter from a major general in Washington who wrote:

Dear Pvt. Green:

I'm sure that your period in the service with the Quartermaster Corps will prove invaluable to you in your new post.

"The funny part about that letter," said Green, "is that it's true. The Army did do me some good."

He told about getting a telephone call late one night from a worried wife whose husband had wired her that his CO wouldn't even let him file for discharge under the Hardship Clause. Green immediately called the CO long distance and asked him what kind of an army camp he thought he was running, telling a soldier such baloney.

"You see," said Green, "now when I talk to an Army brass hat, he can't give me any double talk. I know what goes."

Green's favorite story is about how he was invited by his old CO and some ranking brass to a cocktail party at Camp Lee, shortly after his election. It wasn't long before he had ducked the party and hunted up some of his buddies at his old QM company. They guzzled beer and chewed the fat and they all told Green what he should do in Congress.

They still tell him what to do. One recent letter was from his old first sergeant, now in Egypt, who wrote that if things didn't start improving soon in Congress, he would start cursing Green the way Green used to curse him.

But Green's most faithful correspondent was a guy in the 79th Division in Germany who wrote long weekly letters signed "Foxhole Harry."

Foxhole's first letter was warm and friendly:

Dear Bill:

How are you feeling today? And how are tricks in Washington? Gee, I'll bet the Mrs. and all the kids feel great now that Daddy is a Congressman. Say, Bill, do I have to call you Mr. Congressman or can I call you by your first name. I hope I can call you by your first name.

Besides being friendly and faithful, Foxhole has been Green's best barometer about GI bitching overseas, everything from the point system to the lack of shipping. One of Foxhole's personal bitches concerned Negro soldiers. "We make those colored boys fight," said Foxhole, "but we still don't give them the rights of American first class citizenship. It isn't fair."

Green's mailbag keeps him up to date on civilian bitching, too. To keep his constituents posted and political-minded, Green writes a weekly column for a dozen different suburban papers, telling them just what he's been doing, and why.

But there are still plenty of Philadelphia voters who don't like Green, who don't like anybody who wants to change anything. They even yelled about his proposal for an electric-button system in Congress to cut away the red tape of roll call by doing it in two minutes instead of an hour.

Then there are always cranks like the one who wrote, "You're only a one-term congressman. Roosevelt is dead, Guffey is dying, and you're a dead duck, too. That picture of you on the picket line in the SKF strike finished you for good."

Green explained that he had marched along with the strikers simply because he had believed in what they were striking for, that they were entitled to higher wages because of a higher cost of living.

The ones that do bother him, though, are the letters from people who just won't understand how Congress works, the ones who write, "You big bum. You introduce bills all right, but they never get passed."

"Remember the way it was in the peacetime Army," said Green almost wistfully. "Regular meals, plenty of sleep, lots of passes, no headaches, no problems, no responsibilities. Well, here in Congress, you always got a million things to worry about: a big pile of mail to answer; you're always grabbing a sandwich instead of a meal; you're always fighting to get bills out of committees; and you never know when something's going to pop up and you have to work late."

"But don't get me wrong," said Green, smiling a wide smile. "I prefer Congress. There aren't so many long lines."

"Seems like every time we just finished putting up our tents, we had to pull them down again and move somewhere else. We must have moved at least a dozen times in less than thirty days. But a surgical team is just no good to anybody unless it's right behind the front," said Sgt. Henry Mahnken, of West New York, New Jersey, of 2nd Auxiliary Signal Group. Sometimes he passed the instruments, sometimes he helped the anesthetist, sometimes he subbed as assistant surgeon, holding the belly open while the surgeon cut.

They'd only operate on those patients classified as non-transportable, patients who would die if you moved them. Each such operation was a long, sweating job, three to four hours.

"The war moved so fast that we never knew where it was exactly. But we never had to go anywhere to find it; it always came to us."

23

PRESCRIPTION FOR RECONVERSION

ESTES PARK, COLORADO:

The modern five-bed hospital didn't look as if it had been a saloon only a few months before. The waiting room was full, and the two doctors were busy, the younger doctor setting a small boy's arm, the older one telling a skinny woman to take these pills every day and stop worrying.

The pill-persuader was Dr. Jacob Mall, one of two doctors who stayed behind in the post-tourist season to take care of the town's two thousand permanent residents. The day Mall came home with his Army discharge, 250 townspeople dropped in to say hello.

"This is strictly a social call, Doc, but as long as I'm here I thought I'd tell you that I ain't been feeling so good since you went away. Do you think you can give me a quick once-over, Doc?"

These 250 social calls changed his plans. When he was with a surgical team in New Guinea, he picked up the idea that maybe it would be better for him to specialize again, instead of going back into general practice. He had long talks with other specialists, caught up on all his medical reading, and practically made his decision. There was this standing offer from a big Los Angeles clinic. A wonderful future and the chance to do all kinds of research.

He especially liked the idea because he knew how tough it would be to find an office again and get all the equipment he needed. For all he knew maybe some other doctor had moved in and taken over his practice.

But when he came home he found a town that needed and wanted him, so he said the hell with specializing. Besides, where could you find more beautiful country than Estes Park, even if you have to look at it from the windows of a reconverted saloon?

Mall's young assistant, Dr. C. J. Hipps, wasn't so happy. It was a nice job and Mall himself was a good guy, but general practice just wasn't what he wanted to do. It was like being an office boy when you wanted to be an editor. What he wanted more than anything was a residency in orthopedic surgery. But when he got out of the Navy and wrote to hospitals, they all told him the same thing, "No openings for two years." Still, Hipps had no kick coming. Veterans who got residencies deserved them. Hell, he had never even seen the war.

COLUMBIA, MISSOURI:

When Dr. Jack Gilford suggested to a local landlord that ninety a month was perhaps a little too expensive for a four-room unfurnished apartment without bath or toilet, the landlord gave him a big grin, "G'wan, Doc, you can't kid me. You doctors are coining the money."

Gilford is coining fifty a week at the Ellis Fischel Cancer Hospital, which doesn't seem like too much money for a qualified surgeon with ten years of experience. But Gilford isn't here because of the money. When he went into the Army he divided all his expensive equipment among some doctor friends; when he came back to Cleveland his friends and equipment were scattered all over the world. Then there was a long, futile hunt for an apartment and an office.

But there's more reason than that for his being here. He's here because this is a wonderful opportunity to do mass work and mass good. The surgery he does here in a year would take a lifetime to accumulate in private practice.

Sure, someday he plans to go back to Cleveland and start all over again. Meanwhile here's where he'd like to stay for a while. Now if he could only find an apartment for his family. . . .

SEGUIN, TEXAS:

All their friends told them it was such a silly idea. Who ever heard of two nurses investing their life savings in a twenty-two bed hospital. Everybody knew that small hospitals in small towns were financial white elephants.

But twenty-eight-year-old Dorothea Siepmann knew what she was doing. This was the only hospital in the area. Anyway, a small town hospital went broke only if it was owned by a tiny clique of doctors who wouldn't make it available to other doctors. This hospital would be open to everybody.

She wrote her friend Sarah Hazard all the details. Sarah was a graduate nurse, thinking seriously of becoming a doctor. She and Dorothea had met in an Austin hospital, and they had enlisted in the Army together. She read Dorothea's letter, then forgot all about medical school, grabbed her bankbook and took the next train out.

The two of them only put up three thousand dollars in actual cash. A GI loan guaranteed the rest of the initial payment and they had twenty years to pay thirty thousand dollars.

With the bill of sale officially signed, they went to work. They knocked out a wall, enlarging the nursery and painting it a bright pink. Then they replaced nine old beds, bought an additional six, put in a refrigerator, ordered a new set of dishes, made arrangements to get fresh blood processed cheaply and started buying groceries wholesale instead of retail.

Their hospital opened on Florence Nightingale Day. The whole town sent flowers, the Lions Club promised them an iron lung, and the Elks Club countered with an electrically-controlled incubator.

"We had our first baby five days after we opened," Dorothea said. "We were so excited, we took the woman into the delivery room three times before she finally had it. We just weren't sure any more. I guess we had been in the Army too long."

NEW ORLEANS, LOUISIANA:

Here was this city with a six weeks' waiting list for all hospital beds, and here were five hundred unused beds in a War Surplus Army hospital on the city's outskirts. When Dr. Charles Odom returned and saw all this, he grabbed a telephone. Fifty phone calls later he had a plan and an organization. A plane trip to Washington and a long talk with local bank officials and he had five hundred hospital beds.

Of course, the fact that he had been surgical consultant to the Seventh and Third Armies didn't hurt this football-shouldered surgeon when he went to Washington. And his high professional standing in the city was vital in welding together a non-profit organization of 150 doctors, all of them war veterans.

The present hospital setup won't last. It's being torn down in a few years to make way for a residential district. But the doctors have already made plans to start building a brand-new hospital somewhere in the city, as soon as possible.

"One doctor can't do much," said Odom, "but when there are 150 of us. . . ."

Things couldn't be nicer for navy vet William Bradburn. His residency at this new hospital is just what he wanted. They've given him all kinds of responsibility. Where else would a young resident get a chance to open up an obstetrical ward? Next year when he starts his own practice, he won't have to worry about office space, since he's moving in with his doctor-father. The money headache isn't as bad as it could be because he gets a regular check as an on-the-job-trainee under the GI Bill. It comes in handy when you've got a wife and child and your hospital salary is only thirty-five a month plus maintenance.

So many of his other friends were having it tough. The ones who couldn't get residencies either took jobs teaching science at schools or else went to work for other doctors. The married ones were almost all living with their in-laws.

Bradburn didn't even have an apartment problem. It was all ready and waiting for him when he came home—his father owned it.

TWIN FALLS, IDAHO:

Like a lot of other doctors, Dr. Gordon Dithman Oldham didn't get any special benefits from his years in the Army. As chief of surgery at an Air Corps hospital in Oklahoma, he did enough traumatic operations to fill up a surgical lifetime. But in Twin Falls, he's now just one of the town's twenty-five general practitioners. He may never get to do another traumatic operation as long as he lives.

But Oldham has no regrets. All those doctors who belly-ached about getting rusty in the Army were just lazy, as far as he's concerned. It was up to the doctor whether or not he wanted to fall behind medically. There were always books and medical journals to read, always other doctors to talk to.

His bank account would have been lots fatter if he had stayed home, but then what about all those lawyers and engineers and other professional men who never got a chance to practice what they learned, who never even got to be officers? How could he complain? How could any doctor complain?

"We were living in a house in the outskirts of the city when this Frenchman and his wife came back," said T-3 Bernard Crystal, who was with the engineer liaison section.

"We saw them coming up the hill slowly, both looking a little scared. Then they both suddenly stopped to stare at the house. They must have stood there like that a couple minutes, just staring at the house, staring at all the shrapnel holes and the partially busted roof, just staring, not saying a damn thing. Then the wife pointed to the garden, shaking her head, and the two of them came into the yard and started pulling weeds.

"They told us later it was their house. The Germans had kicked them out and they hadn't been back for three years.

"I'll never forget the way they were pulling out those weeds."

24

HOMELESS VETS, INC.

You can see them there every Sunday afternoon. They come to these twenty-five acres of barren land at Salt Lake City's outskirts.

The man paces off his lot's boundary, counting aloud, his eyes almost closed. Then the young woman points to some invisible furniture in an invisible room and decides to put it somewhere else. But the man says no. They'll argue. And in the middle of the argument, they'll both pause, then burst out laughing. Nobody watches them. Everybody else on the twenty-five acres is doing the same thing.

Everybody else means 106 veterans and their families, all of them incorporated in a non-profit, $750,000 housing project of their own, under the title, "Homeless Vets, Inc."

On lot 65, Jack Morton told how the dream grew out of desperation. How a few of them went from big-shot banker to big-shot contractor to big-shot architect, and everybody said, yes, sir, we sure are willing to do everything in our power to help you boys, but right now our hands are tied. You know the situation. Shortage of materials. Tough to get labor. You know how it is.

The few grew to twenty veterans who couldn't afford to pay fifteen thousand dollars for a four-thousand-dollar home. They thought they could buy tax-delinquent land cheap. But during the war, city and county officials had grabbed everything they could for themselves.

Still, they did find other people who wanted to help. An architect who handed them absolutely free fifteen different completely detailed sets of plans and specifications. The president of the Interstate Brick Company promised them all the bricks they needed. The Union Trust Company said: "If the land's good, we'll finance it." The Plumbers Union told them: "If any of the plumbers slack on the job, fire them. We'll get you others. And we'll show you how to save money buying supplies."

They even found land. But it was a big tract and they figured they'd need at least a hundred veterans on the deal. So they put a small notice in the *Salt Lake Tribune*, "Any veteran interested in having his own home. . . ."

The hall was packed. Morton and Joe O'Carroll explained the plan. Anybody interested?

Anybody interested!

For the next few weeks, from dawn to midnight, the eleven elected members of the board constantly picked up their phones to hear, "Well, how are we doing?"

They were doing fine. With every member pledging $500, they bought a twenty-five acre tract just outside the city limits, on the slope of a hill with a fifty-mile view of the valley. It cost $38,000, about $355 apiece. Their nearest neighbor paid $1200 for his single lot. They were saving money already. The county had promised to make the roads, if they'd pay for the oil. Their contractor was twenty-seven-year-old navy vet Hamer Culp. This was his biggest job—he had only built two homes before. But he was smart and hard-working and they had faith in him. Instead of a whopping commission, he only wanted $400 a month.

The *Tribune* ran a big aerial picture of the tract with the caption, "THIS IS THEIR HUNK OF AMERICA."

Several days later there was another picture of several smiling faces, saying, "ALL THEY NEED NOW IS MA-TERIALS."

Soil pipes, rock lathes, hardwood flooring, fixtures, shingles, doors, mill work. . . .

They all chipped in to send Hamer Culp to Washington to talk to housing expeditor Wilson Wyatt. It seemed to them that veterans who built homes should have the same priority as the F.P.H.A. gave to those who rented.

But several days later Culp came back. "The only thing I accomplished was to see a good ball game." Why? Too much red tape. Too much fear that a change in priorities now would upset the whole housing apple cart.

They had general meetings to discuss everything. They wanted to have a choice of floor plans and elevations as well as freedom to make the house brick or concrete or frame. They didn't want Veterans Heights to look like a row of corn. How about curved roads? Good idea. Say, what about calling those twin streets Scotch and Soda?

There was also the prolonged discussion on whether they should remain as part of the county or petition to be included in the city.

"How about the sewage and fire protection?"

"If we stick with the county, our taxes are lower, aren't they?"

Finally, a vet who waved his hand excitedly, his face all red, said: "I don't think we should attach ourselves to the county. I saw one child running around loose with chicken pox! I don't want *my* kid to get it." And the explosion of laughter in the room.

"The woodwork is going to be light cream," said Mrs. James Croft on lot 9. "And the kitchen will be two-tone. We've even started shopping."

"Yeah, we bought a bedroom set." They smiled.

Everything was all planned, they said. They even knew exactly where the end tables and lamps would be.

"The way we're talking, I guess people will think we're moving right in. Of course, it'll be months yet. But they are starting to dig out the basement tomorrow. I guess nobody can really blame us for being a little excited. We never had a home of our own before." His wife grinned.

On lot 89, Rodney Day still couldn't get over the fact that he had paid eight hundred dollars for a two-piece living-room set. "Lucky I was a captain and could save some money. I've got a pretty good job, too." He knew lots of guys who weren't so lucky. Some had to drop out because they couldn't raise the six to eight thousand dollars, or because another baby was on the way.

"You ought to see the letters we've received from veterans all over the country," said solemn-speaking Keith Webb on lot 68. As secretary of the corporation, Keith had to tell inquiring vets how to duplicate the setup.

"We also get these heartbreaking letters from fellas who want to join us. But all we can do is put them on our list in case somebody drops out. It's a long list."

No, they hadn't bought anything yet. They were waiting for prices to go down a little.

"Besides, we do have a few things of our own," answered Keith.

His wife laughed, "Sure, a radio and a card table."

Somebody yelled "Hiya, neighbor" and they got together to talk. Eldon and Betty Southam on lot 7 looked a little envious when Roy Austin on lot 2 proudly described how they were already pouring concrete into his basement. They talked about electric outlets, different shades of brick, making a box for the milk, building garages, and whether to grow strawberries or raspberries.

They mentioned how ecstatic the Milzareks were on lot 1. Who wouldn't be after living in a tent on an empty lot? And what about the good news of the arrival of seventy thousand feet of lumber, enough for ten homes? Everybody said they'd have thirty roofs up by Christmas, didn't they?

"We hope," added Eldon. "We fondly fervently hope."

Soon they were all talking bedrooms and living rooms and somebody volunteered that the best system he heard of was the one with "spheres of influence." The husband gets the final word about plans for the bathroom, living room, and basement. And the wife is the dictator for the kitchen, bedroom, and hall.

At the subdivision the next morning, building supervisor Hamer Culp tried to smile when he talked about the women with their single-spaced typewritten sheets of questions and suggestions. Then, after everything was settled, the parents would come in and tell them what they *really* wanted. Finally they would drop the whole matter in Culp's lap, everybody glaring and asking, "Now, what do you think, Hamer?" And Hamer would smile weakly, "It's all a matter of taste. . . ."

What got him, though, were the telephone calls in the middle of the night to tell him they had decided to move the chimney or put in another door somewhere.

"I know it's their first house," moaned Hamer. "But oh, my God. . . ."

The tanks got all the headlines. No matter what newspaper you picked up, the tanks got all the headlines.

Okay. Good.

But the infantry was there, too. Infantry sprawled all over the tops of tanks, riding a hundred miles a day that way sometimes, acting as the eyes and ears for the blind tank. Flushing out housetop snipers, hopping off to clean out an AT gun hiding around the curve, deploying to wipe out a roadblock. Sitting naked on top of tanks. . . .

Still, they were lucky in a way; they were riding. There were all those infantry divisions who walked, long forced marches into booby-trapped towns, through mine fields—and always there were snipers, snipers, and more snipers. The dirty job of mop-up that never made any headlines, seldom crept into any stories.

Walking for miles and miles and days and days until your feet were dead and your body was lead and your mind kept mumbling, "I'm so goddam tired. . . ."

25

TAXI TRUSTBUSTERS

"THIS is for me," said the young cab driver, smiling and stretching in front of Chicago's Wrigley Building. "Nobody telling me what to do. If I want to knock off for a couple hours, I knock off. No time clocks, no bosses, and the dough's good. So you can put down in your magazine that Tony De Salvo formerly of the United States Army is now a very happy guy."

Neon-blazing on the dark, deserted street a few blocks away, just off Michigan Boulevard, was a cafeteria called Pixley's. Most of the parked cabs were Yellow or Checker, only a few were marked, "Chicago Veterans Cabs." Inside the half-empty cafeteria, the cab drivers were mixed and scattered: a few older ones, sitting by themselves, brooding over their coffee; a beardless blond wearing a discharge button rubbing his eyes, then sleepily sipping his chocolate soda; and, in the rear of the place, a small group loudly discussing the ways of the world.

From the atom bomb to Truman to sex:

"I picked up a salesman at Union Station today, and honest, I hated to see him get out. He just came back from Florida and was busting with stories about the women down there. . . ."

Before another coffee, the talk turned to the cab business. Of course business was wonderful now in cab-hungry Chicago, but how long was it going to last? Eighteen months? Two years? Then what? Back to making peanuts again, $25 a week instead of $125.

"Comes the bust, a lot of you young guys are gonna want to get out of this racket," warned one of the older men.

"Sure I'm gonna get out," said a red-headed vet. "I don't go for this business of driving a car all night long. Now I'm not bitching, because the dough's swell. But I'm a married man. My wife likes me to come home at night."

The place was loud with laughter.

They talked and talked. The discussion seemed to center around the veterans now. One of them said that as soon as cab fares slowed up, he was going to take advantage of the GI Bill and learn all about television. Another told how this cab-driving was paying for his new home. And a third vet started comparing Chicago cabs with London cabs and suddenly he was remembering all the good times he had in Piccadilly.

You could feel the envy in the eyes of the other men.

The group around the table kept breaking up and reforming with different faces and voices. But the veterans were still in the spotlight. Especially the one who spilled out some of the plans of the Chicago Veterans Cab Association: a big new garage to service the cabs, more parking stands all over the city, and in every cab, two-way radio contact with the office.

There was just the slightest trace of bitterness in a cabbie's voice when he said, "I'll tell you this much. The cops would still be arresting you guys and you'd never get to first base in this town if you weren't veterans."

At the soda fountain, an eager-looking man told the full story of how the Veterans Cab Association grew from six guys operating out of their buddy's gas station to six hundred angry men who drove to Washington to put their case before the American people.

Their case was simple. They didn't want to drive for the

Yellow and the Checker outfits. They wanted their own organization. But the Yellow and the Checker people had sewed up the city in an agreement giving them a virtual monopoly of the three thousand available licenses—just as they had done in fifty-seven other cities.

So when the veterans came out in their own cabs with the ruptured ducks painted on the doors, the city turned thumbs down on license applications and the cops pulled them in.

But the word spread and soon the vets had their own pressure group: not money, but people.

". . . I think it's a darn shame the way you boys have been getting a runaround since you got back. If my husband were alive, he'd be right with you. He was killed in Tunisia. . . ."

Politicians got worried. Six hundred veterans and their families, friends, and sympathizers could be translated into votes. And this was an election year.

When the newspapers picked it up, the people's talk grew even louder:

"Is this the way Chicago treats its veterans? Slap them on the back and kick them in the pants at the same time?"

"Well, wait awhile," was the politicians' answer. "We'll figure something out."

But the six hundred vets didn't want to wait.

A cab caravan packed with veterans and their families moving east along Route 30 to Washington:

Warsaw, Ft. Wayne, Delphos ". . . You folks don't have to worry about places to sleep. We heard you were coming and everything's all fixed up. . . ."

Upper Sandusky, Bucyrus, Massillon ". . . The candy's for the kids and women; the cigarettes, for the men. Hope there's enough to go around. . . . Money? Are you trying to insult us? . . ."

East Liverpool, Pittsburgh ". . . Just to make sure you boys don't have any traffic trouble, we've been delegated to convoy you right through. . . . No thanks needed; we're veterans ourselves. . . ."

Greensburg, McConnellsburg, Gettysburg ". . . Honest to God, fellas, so you ate a little food in my restaurant, it's not gonna break me. . . . Let's not argue about it, the treat's on me. . . ."

In Washington, the Army had prepared part of Camp Simms for them to move into; the Red Cross put up enough money to start a camp kitchen; and a near-by gas station poured 250 gallons of gas into their tanks, saying, "Forget it. It's free. And there's more where that came from."

There were lots of stories about them in the newspapers, stories and pictures and sympathy. At the Department of Justice, officials made careful notes about their monopoly charges against Checker and Yellow, and promised action. After that, important, interested government big-shots saw the cab-drivers' delegation, listened thoughtfully, made some telephone calls.

About a week later they got the good news. If they went back to Chicago, the cops wouldn't arrest them any more. But the big surprise back in Chicago was the discovery that their best friends were now the politicians and aldermen. The politicians had felt the public pulse and changed direction. It wasn't long before the vets had 275 licenses and promises of 375 more. Of course, there was a joker attached. The licenses were only temporary and could be recalled without warning or reason at any time. So maybe someday, when public pressure eased off. . . .

Meanwhile, dozens of vets found themselves with their cabs all painted, ready to go, and no license. The promised 375 licenses had been pigeonholed. "What was I gonna do?" complained one of the "bandit" drivers. "Wait all year until the aldermen decided to give me a license? I got two kids. . . ."

Back at the group table in Pixley's, a fat driver argued in a twangy voice with one of the vets. "Now don't get me wrong. You guys have just as much a right to make a living as me. All I'm griping about is that the public don't know that a lot of us guys driving Checker and Yellow cabs are also vets, just like you. . . ."

It was past three o'clock in the morning and the group table was still forming and reforming but always full.

Out in the quiet street, you walked several long dead blocks before you found a cab waiting patiently on State Street. Inside, thirty-nine-year-old Jack Krezar talked philosophically about the cab business.

"I bought this cab from a woman out in Riverside. It belonged to her husband who never got to be a veteran. He was killed in the Pacific.

"And do you know why I bought this cab? Because when I came home with my discharge, I spent almost an hour trying to get a cab to stop for me. I was so damn mad at cab drivers. . . ."

He smiled. "There was another small reason. The jewelry-selling business isn't what it used to be."

Still, he didn't like hacking because there was too much rush-rush. He was thirty-nine and wanted something more settled and permanent.

But there was something about this whole veterans' cab fight in Chicago that excited him, the idea that six hundred veterans with no money could crack into a million-dollar monopoly.

"Because here's the thing," said Jack. "If we vets can do it here in Chicago, there's no reason why vets can't do it somewhere else, is there?"

In some places it was spontaneous—like two grenades thrown in the same hole at the same time. The Americans grabbed the Russians and the Russians grabbed the Americans, everybody shaking hands and laughing and opening bottles of vodka and slapping each other on the back. Everything friendliness bubbling over. Amerikanski, Russky, tovarich. . . . How about trading me that red star on your hat for a good old American dollar bill. . . . Will you sign my short snorter? . . . Say, this vodka stuff is really potent, ain't it? . . .

26

THE TIME IS NOW

THE professor was still in bed Sunday morning when a student banged on the door, barged in excitedly, "Did you really mean what you said about me running for Congress?"

Professor Herman Schneurer blinked sleepily. "Why, of course."

They had talked about it over some beers the night before at Glenn's Cafe. It had started with a discussion about Clarence Brown, their representative for the Seventh Congressional District.

"I just got an answer from him about a Walter Lippmann column I sent him. He warned me not to read such radical columnists. Walter Lippmann a radical. . . . God Almighty."

So they talked about Brown, how he had voted against the defense of Guam, against the absentee ballot for soldiers, even against free lunches for poor school kids.

"And we can't even get anybody to oppose him," said the Professor, who had the side jobs of Democratic county committeeman and CIO *News* editor.

"Say, how about you, Fessenden. How would you like to run for Congress?"

"Me? Are you kidding?"

Candidate for Congress! What the hell did he know about

politics? Just some stuff he had read in a textbook, heard in an Antioch College classroom, read in the newspapers.

He didn't even know if he could make a speech. Probably start stammering or blushing or something. And what did he have to say? Tell how he won the war single-handed as a public relations captain in the First Army? Or that he was twenty-six years old and wanted a brave new world?

Or what? That he knew damn well he didn't have the faintest remotest chance of beating the tightly organized Brown Republican machine?

Then why go through the motions? Why beat your head against a stone wall? He could have such a wonderful time finishing college, going on picnics with his wife Susan, leisurely enjoying being back in Yellow Springs again.

But, damn it, this was more important. This was Paul Robeson making a speech in the auditorium about Negro soldiers who didn't want to come back to America.

This was his friend talking about the atom bomb, saying, "Sure, Bruce, I know the world's going to hell. But until it does, I'm gonna have a good time. Anyway, what can *we* do about it?"

This was Susan speaking, Susan who made tank thermostats during the war and unionized her shop: "Bruce, we can't leave politics to the politicians. We've got to make ourselves heard and felt. This is our government."

That's why.

Shake hands with everybody, smile, keep repeating your name. See this guy, see that guy. That old man over there is the contact man for his whole county. Be nice to him. Don't compromise yourself. Don't tell him anything you don't honestly believe. But be nice to him. And when you write a publicity release, stick your name in every paragraph. Fish fries, women's clubs, churches, speeches, speeches, speeches. One county to another county. . . . Greene, Clark, Clinton, Champaign, Warren, Logan, Fayette, Madison, Union. . . .

Whom should I speak to? Whom should I convince? What should I say?

He learned fast.

Another Democratic candidate had sneaked in under the deadline. A man named Ehl who had been running for years. He was the kind of guy who came to Democratic party dinners dressed in his American Legion uniform and, instead of making a campaign speech, simply stood up, saluted, sat down. Now, with the war over, he had changed his tactics. Instead of saluting, he had a one-sentence speech. It was:

"I am for 100 per cent Americanism."

The campaign got discouraging. Of the forty-three newspapers in the county, only two printed any news of the primary. But the big thing was the apathy of the people. They just didn't care. At one Democratic rally where they even had a boxing match and entertainment scheduled, only twelve people showed up.

Then the whispering campaigns:

Bzzzz, bzzz . . . Don't vote for Fessenden. He's from that college in Yellow Springs. Everybody knows how radical the whole town is.

Don't vote for Fessenden. Even if he's elected he won't be able to take office for a few years because he's so young.

Imagine that Fessenden plugging things like OPA and FEPC. He's a Communist, I tell ya.

There were other things. Susan didn't dare to smoke a cigarette at the Jackson Day dinner because it might cause comment, lose votes. And how embarrassed she was when she was asked to lead an audience in singing "America" and she had to sing a solo on the second stanza because nobody else knew the words.

But mostly it was trying not to explode when people walked up to him and said things like, "Don't you agree with me, young feller, that Senator Taft's Health Bill is downright socialistic?"

"You've got to be careful of everything you do and say to people, Bruce. . . . Everything means votes."

More speeches. Pass out pamphlets at the factories. The workers will listen. Don't mention your opponent's name; it gives him free publicity. People sometimes forget what you say and just remember his name. Don't forget, the county committee expects a donation. The newspapers expect you to advertise. Two speeches and two chicken dinners in one night. Speak louder, more clearly. Project your personality. You've got to sell yourself, Fessenden. . . .

You've got to sell yourself to those of the 302,000 in this gerrymandered Ohio district who will come out and vote in the Democratic party primary. About 8,000 maybe. And a lot of them are retired, individualistic farmers who don't believe a lot of things you believe. Besides, you haven't got a chance, you know. Except for the 1936 landslide, this district has always been conservative and Republican.

The primary returns came in slowly. The vote was heavier than the last primary and Fessenden carried four out of nine counties but he lost to Ehl by slightly more than a thousand votes.

Why?

Didn't see enough people . . . didn't make enough speeches . . . the people didn't care . . . they remembered Ehl's name from previous campaigns . . . the whispering campaigns.

"Well, Bruce? Discouraged?"

"Discouraged? Why should I be? We'll be stronger in the next primary. I've got a lot of new contacts to pass onto the next PAC candidate. A lot of suggestions too. He'll have to start out earlier than I did, see more people, profit by my mistakes, make more speeches. That's all. It'll take time. . . ."

Time. How much time? How much time is there before inflation, depression, atomic bombs, war?

"Susan, you know what? We've got to write to all our friends. We've got to buttonhole every liberal we know. We've got to keep saying it until we say it in our sleep—get into politics. . . . get into politics. If you don't run for office, find out who does. Write to him, talk to him, tell him what you think. Join your local political party clubs. Pass on the word. Talk. Write. Vote. If there was ever a time in our history to get politically excited, the time is now. . . ."

When the British ship pulled slowly into port, all the news-papermen crowded inside because it was the first boat back from the beach. The boat was loaded with dead and wounded. One of the wounded talked quickly, excitedly.

He told how he got soaking wet wading ashore with a load of explosives on his back. He was part of a demolition team of twenty-eight who were supposed to blow gaps in the con-crete wall.

"I was just coming out of the water when this guy exploded right in front of me. There just wasn't anything left of him except some of his skin which splattered all over my arm. I remember dipping my arm in the water to wash it off. I guess I was too excited to be scared."

Then he told how they blew a tank barricade and he got hit in the elbow with a hunk of shrapnel.

"It wasn't as tough as I thought it would be," he said.

The other soldiers in the hold of the ship didn't say any-thing. The war was still in their faces.

27

THIS IS OUR OWN

"I just can't understand it," said the maid at the Hotel Fort Des Moines. "This convention's been going on for almost three days now and I ain't seen a single drunk yet."

No drunks, no water-filled paper bags thrown out of windows, no hotfoots, no parades, no "Auld Lang Syne."

Instead, an ex-Wac fell fast asleep in her chair after forty-eight straight hours of work, two dozen members of a platform sub-committee worked until dawn, took showers, ate breakfast, went back to work again.

"A benzedrine salesman would clean up a fortune around here."

Tuscaloosa, Yuba City, Cheyenne, San Diego, Brooklyn, and 1600 delegates of 526 chapters of the American Veterans Committee coming to their first constitutional convention.

It was all so new to them. So many had never belonged to any organization before. And they had never dreamed of being part of a smoke-filled caucus, or jumping up and down and waving their hands, getting overheated about a word or a phrase or an involved piece of parliamentary procedure.

"Point of information, Mr. Chairman. . . ."

And if they seemed silly or juvenile sometimes, arguing about pointless technicalities—you checked your smiles. Because no matter what else, no matter how confused and groping it sometimes seemed, you knew that the room was filled with sincerity.

The sincerity of intelligent veterans, representing every shade of liberalism, who wildly cheered Bishop Bernard Shiel's opening convention speech, "We want a new world; we want a fresh start; we want another chance to make our world worth living in."

But the question here in Des Moines was, where did AVC fit in? What were they going to be, how were they going to act, who was going to lead them?

If you wandered in and out of the hotel rooms, the caucuses and the clusters of conversation, you got a confused patchwork picture. From the tone of the talk, you couldn't be sure whether this was going to be a birthday party or a funeral.

This was plain: they were scared. They were scared that right here and now the whole AVC might split into a lot of stupid political splinters.

There was no conflict about Bolte. Everybody wanted him back as chairman of AVC. The fight was for the vice-chairmanship.

It was this fight, between Gilbert Harrison and Fred Borden, that threatened to crack the whole AVC wide open at the seams.

That night when the two candidates went from caucus to caucus to explain themselves, the delegates were ready to boil down their area of difference with specific questions:

Was there any conflict between them about the AVC platform favoring O.P.A. extension, F.E.P.C., civilian control of the atomic bomb, the Wyatt Housing Bill, the Murray Full Employment Bill?

Naturally not.

Did they both believe in the AVC creed, "Citizens first, veterans second"?

[228]

Why, of course.

Then what?

Well, said Borden, I think Harrison's aim at five million membership is strictly crackpot. AVC can only be important if it remains a strong instrument of progressive action. But if we take in that many members, we're going to have to water down our platform to please everybody and we'll only have a lot of empty words left. Besides I think we can be a lot more militant than we have been.

I hate red-baiting, said Harrison, because it makes us fight among ourselves when we should be fighting people like Gerald K. Smith. But the simple fact is that Borden and his group have been plainly identified with the extreme left wing. And right now all America is watching us, waiting to see what we do. And if Borden and his group get in, the whole American press and people will pin the red tag on us and the political effectiveness of AVC won't be worth two cents.

Two more questions. If the cleavage between their two groups reaches a point where it might mean the bust-up of AVC, would they both resign in favor of a third candidate? Borden said yes; Harrison shook his head furiously, said no. There was an angry howl.

Last question. Borden had told how he had attended every National Planning Committee meeting. Had he ever once made any criticism or suggestion there? Borden hesitated, said no. There was a long pause.

Up in his room, Harrison tried to explain himself. Quitting in favor of a third candidate would only be dodging the issue. It would only mean a continuance of confusion. This issue had to be met head-on. Both the AVC and the American people had a right to know where AVC was headed for.

Franklin D. Roosevelt, Jr., seconded that. He didn't think Borden was a Communist, but he was supported by the Communists and identified with their platform. If they got control, they wouldn't represent the whole of AVC; they'd simply represent an extreme faction and AVC would wither and die.

In the hotel lobby, Fred Borden sounded tired and subdued. Some delegates were beginning to think he wore horns, he said. Okay, he was left of Harrison and Roosevelt, he wanted a more militant AVC, he believed in certain platform planks that they didn't. So what? He wasn't forcing anything down anybody's throat. This was a democratic organization. The delegates would vote for whom and what they wanted. As for the red herring, it was just a phony issue to scare away the uncommitted delegates. What's more, he had always believed in the unity of AVC and while he might withdraw his candidacy, he would never bolt; he was going to stay in and fight for what he believed in.

To all this, the delegates listened and wondered. Of the flood of handouts, there was a single yellow mimeographed sheet by a Chicago delegate who expressed the general worry and confusion. "Many of us have been disgusted and disillusioned by the spectacle of internal dissension. . . . I am just an average member . . . I can't understand why we have to come to such a terrible crossroads . . . The AVC must not be rent asunder. . . . We must keep faith. . . ."

We must keep faith. . . .

"Say, did you hear what happened? That café across the street refused to serve two Negro delegates."

Minutes later AVC was united again, a block-long picket line in front of the store with the delegates chanting, "Jim Crow Must Go. . . . Jim Crow Must Go. . . ."

No more confusions of factions. This was basic and simple. Only a few hours before they had put it into their platform, "We oppose . . . all forms of racial discrimination. We for-

bid it in our own ranks and we shall fight it in law and in practice wherever it is found. . . ."

"Jim Crow Must Go. . . ." Not just a lot of pretty-sound-
ing words in a convention platform. They meant what they
said.

When the cops came, it took delegate Frank Williams five
minutes of firm politeness and convincing before the police
captain finally agreed that there was a city ordinance against
any discrimination and that the café manager should be arrested not Monday, but immediately.

Six Des Moines veterans watched and listened to the whole
thing.

"Say, you guys are really doing something. How do we join?"

But inside the committee rooms, discussions were heated.
The bonus defeated, draft extension shelved, world government compromised. There was also a labor plank amendment
which supported the right of all organized labor to unionize
any or all workers anywhere in these United States. One group
wanted to tack on, "especially in the South." It was defeated
only after a Louisiana delegate read part of a letter from CIO's
Van Bittner warning that such an AVC plank would hurt
much more than help.

At the final session of the nominating committee, the add-
ing machine clicked away, nervously narrowing the margin of
difference between Harrison and Norris Helford. Borden had
dramatically withdrawn his candidacy and his backers
switched to Helford.

It looked close, and it was. Harrison leading Helford by
several hundred votes, with Bob White, the third candidate,
holding the balance of power with his five thousand votes.

Until the final balloting, the hotel was full of rumors and
whispers. Where would the five thousand go? Finally it was
announced. To Harrison.

On the train to St. Louis, an elderly colonel listened to the still-excited delegates rehashing the whole convention. Suddenly he interrupted. "How come you men didn't join the Legion?"

The four AVC delegates turned to stare.

"Why should we?"

The colonel paused. "Well, after all, we spent a lot of time and money building up the Legion. All we're asking you young men to do is to step in and take over."

The men were full of silence for a minute and the train noises sounded loud and sharp. Then one of the younger delegates spoke up. "Look, colonel, this is our own organization. AVC represents all the progressive democratic things we believe in and the Legion doesn't, that's all."

The colonel froze and there was silence again and finally somebody started a discussion on the comparative merits of the Dodgers and Cardinals.

House-cleaning a town always means sudden death for some-body. It means kicking a door in, lobbing in a grenade fast, and then running in to see who's still alive and who wants to surrender and who wants to die. Then it means yelling upstairs for the bastards to come down and give up. If nobody answers it means creeping upstairs to double-check, throwing up an-other grenade, praying like hell that there isn't any Jerry with a waiting grenade in his hand hiding in the bedroom or the closet or the toilet.

And when one house is cleaned out, there's another house and another house and another house.

28

NEW ORLEANS MUCKRAKER

For New Orleans, it was a date for the history book. Young Mayor Morrison knew it. So did the Old Regulars and the gamblers. But a lot of citizens didn't. To them it was just another dull election about some bond issue or something. Besides, how do they expect you to go out and vote when it's raining so hard?

But for the ones who knew, it was the answer to the big question: who gets elected in 1950, Reform or Corruption?

In the past fifty years, New Orleans hasn't only been "the eatingest, drinkingest, paradingest city in the country" but also one of the most politically corrupt. There had been only one reform mayor in all that time, and he had lasted a single term. It was the pat formula for politics that Lincoln Steffens had publicized a long time ago: corruption gets so bad in a city that the citizens finally rise up to kick out the machine and elect an honest guy. But then their excitement dies down, the people settle back and forget about politics, and in the next election the well-organized machine sweeps right back in again.

April 15 was the big test. The cards seemed to be all stacked against Morrison. It had been a year since the flower-covered cabs streamed down St. Charles Avenue, honking their horns, people throwing confetti, waving flags, cheering the ten bands that paraded up and down in front of the old City Hall. A year since handsome war veteran de Lesseps Story ("Chep") Morrison had surprised everybody, especially himself, by beating the unbeatable Maestri machine, last Louisiana remnant of Huey Long. That day Morrison had told the wildly applauding crowd something they thought was very funny: that if he did everything he had to do, lots of them would be booing instead of cheering him within a year.

And he was right. He had house-cleaned the city's corruption so completely that he seemed to have stepped hard on almost everybody's toes. His first post-election suggestion—that the city legalize gambling to rid itself of gangsters and add some seven million dollars to its income—that horrified the women's organizations and the preachers. Some of the businessmen got mad because they couldn't buy political favors any more, hotel owners became indignant when Board of Health inspectors actually started enforcing the law, and night club owners yelled bloody murder when Morrison withdrew cops who had acted as their private bouncers. Housewives complained when he didn't cut the sales tax, real estate owners didn't like the plans for equitable tax reassessment, and reformers were disturbed when Chep cut off a thousand political deadheads—wasn't he technically tampering with civil service?

Even his father-in-law didn't like him anymore. His father-in-law, James Waterman, operated, among other things, a racing sheet. When Morrison put the city's seven thousand bookies out of business, that hit Waterman where it hurt—his bankbook. In fact, Waterman got so mad, he even instituted recall proceedings against his son-in-law.

But the most discouraging complaints came from the 262 precinct captains in Morrison's own brand-new political organization. They wanted patronage. The big downtown wards complained that the smaller uptown wards were getting too many jobs and the uptown wards complained they weren't getting enough. The truth was, all the Maestri men had been frozen in their jobs, without tests, by a new civil service law (which Morrison himself had introduced in the state legislature).

So here he was, his organization discontented, his popularity at a low ebb, and the all-decisive bond issue coming up. Morrison was no dumbhead. He knew that the only hope to keep reform government in New Orleans was to show the voters something tangible. Not a bank balance or a moral cleanup or fine, fancy words, but physical things like a modern civic center, badly needed street repairs, a central Union Station combining the city's scattered railroad stations, underpasses and overpasses. That's what the bond issues provided, $23,500,-000 for just those things. Tied in with all that were other plans for a deepwater canal to double the port facilities, more playgrounds, parks, schools, quadrupled trade and air traffic.

That's what it meant: everything.

It was a tight squeeze. With the heavy rain and the light vote, the bond issues barely passed. The front-page cartoon in the *Item* the next day showed a man representing New Orleans wiping the anxious sweat from his face. The caption was, "Whew."

The voter's okay meant a lot of things. It meant that the five thousand unemployed gamblers around town could give up the ghost and start looking for other jobs. The ten thousand prostitutes, who once had their own police-protected cabstands, would have to move to greener pastures. No more graft-worries for the old grocer who once complained to Chep that a detective had forced him to put a slot machine in his store, and that he had to pay off the detective, the police sergeant, and the cop on the beat. New Orleans was in for a political and physical face-lifting. As for Boss Maestri, he might as well take his million dollars and go down to Florida to relax; he's through.

Maestri first became mayor back in 1936 when Huey Long was still the Louisiana Kingfish. Huey wasn't very satisfied with the New Orleans mayor then, and Maestri simply suggested that he'd like to be mayor. Maestri had been one of the big-money boys behind Huey in the early days, so Huey slapped him on the back and said, why sure.

Maestri didn't like to make speeches, his grammar was so bad. So rather than put him through the ordeal of an election, Huey grandly instructed his robot state legislature to pass laws stripping all the powers from the incumbent mayor. That finally persuaded the mayor to quit. Huey then appointed his friend Maestri to take over, extending his term from four to six years and giving him dictatorial powers of absolute veto and appointment.

To help out still further, Huey made a trip to New York to invite Slot Machine King Frankie Costello to come down and take over. That provided Huey with enough money for "worthy causes" and gave Maestri lots of new friends to influence people.

The annual slot machine take alone each year added up to an estimated three million dollars in addition to the heavy shakedown from pimps, gamblers, lottery boys, bookies, and the rest of the flourishing tenderloin. Maestri never had to worry about his slush fund. But Maestri himself didn't handle the rake-off; the royal family of fifty police captains did that.

What Maestri did was to act as the Big Power. He operated a "potkettle" budget; whenever you need money—dip in. Maestri dipped in to the tune of two hundred thousand dollars a year for needy pressure groups, who guaranteed lots of votes. As a special service, the Boss lent his cops to hotels to act as house detectives. He was most generous with his cops during a strike. His blackjack-swinging police made the dock strike a bloody page in the city's history. During the cab strike, the Boss ordered a cop to drive in the front seat with every scabbing driver.

When the Kingfish was killed, the state machine cracked quickly. By 1940, the People's League of Independent Voters had swept Sam Jones into the governor's office. Elected to the state legislature in the same sweep was a twenty-nine-year-old lawyer, Chep Morrison.

Chep acted as House whip for Jones and soon earned a reputation as a bright boy with a hard mind. He attacked so much opposition legislation that when a bill came up concerning sweet potatoes, and Chep kept quiet, an opposition legislator jumped up and said, "At last we have a subject in which the gentleman from New Orleans has no interest."

Maestri's first political opposition came when the Independent Citizens Group organized in 1945. They were well-heeled and highly organized but they had no candidate to run against Maestri. They finally settled on navy veteran Joe Fernandez, who had once run for congressman on the opposition ticket, and lost. Stocky Scott Wilson, now Morrison's right-hand brain-truster, warned them they had picked a lemon, that Fernandez would sell out. Sure enough, Fernandez announced that he didn't feel like running against Maestri six weeks before primary time. The double cross was so raw, it even made a lot of "unpolitical" citizens mad enough to want to vote.

Left high and dry, the Independents sent out a dozen wires to people to please be their candidate for mayor. With so many Costello mobsters in town, it was unhealthy to say yes, and nobody did. That's where Chep Morrison came in. A lieutenant colonel in an overseas port battalion outfit, he had just been discharged. He was all set to take his wife and baby son on a long vacation when the Independents heard he was in town and swarmed in with the high pressure. The next morning they had a candidate.

Chep was a natural: good record; handsome; young; old respected family; war background.

The veterans organized for him and held big rallies, fifteen hundred of them volunteering as poll watchers. The women groups consolidated, rang doorbells, and paraded through town carrying brooms and posters saying, "Sweep the city clean!" The town's three newspapers, which had supported Maestri in the W.P.A. days, now blasted him daily. With the strikebreaking days fresh in mind, labor went solid for Chep.

Chep hit hard when he spoke. He picked up Maestri's slogan of "Don't rock the boat" and threw it right back at him. "Don't rock the boat. Don't disturb reconversion. Reconvert from what? From foul to fouler? From slippery to slick?"

For the ministers Chep had this message: "You preach a lot but you don't vote. My enemies are active enemies and I need your active help to win."

He got plenty of active help. But he himself was his biggest asset. Before breakfast he was at the trolley-car barns for the change in shift to talk to the workers. "My name is Morrison." Then he had a smile and personality the women really went for. The Colonial Dames postponed their annual meeting so it wouldn't interfere with registration at the polls. The *Times Picayune* featured the primary on its society page as the main social event of the day. In one precinct where a man died before he could vote, his wife came to the polls later in the day with her two brothers. "I'm doing this for Charley," she said. She was also doing it for Chep. He carried that precinct by three votes.

As Maestri put it to the press:

"Them women beat me."

Sitting in a barber shop at the St. Charles Hotel the day after election, Chep heard the barber say to another customer, "I was sure surprised when that young feller beat Maestri." And Chep took the towel off his face, sat up and said, "So was I, brother, so was I."

Once in, Chep worked fast. One of his first official acts was to give up the mayor's power of absolute veto and appointment, leaving final approval again in the hands of the democratic majority of the five commissioners.

"I did that because such power is dangerous, no matter who has it. And I won't always be mayor."

Then he repealed an ordinance. The week before election, he had been talking to one of the Independent cab drivers, asking how business was.

"Not so hot. Can't even get equal privileges at hotel hackstands. Yellow Cab's got the monopoly."

"That's not fair. The streets are public. If I get elected, I'll get that fixed up."

"Think so?"

"I think so."

Next on his little list, were the police. First, Morrison appointed a tough combat colonel as police superintendent. As soon as Chep announced the appointment, the air corps colonel who had directed the vets for Morrison flipped over to Maestri's side; he had wanted that job. Even more unhappy were the four hundred cops. They were rotated like pinwheels; all their graft tieups were continuously broken before they could set up new ones. Besides rotating them, their new boss sent them through a special tough training course which weeded out a lot. Big fat cops who had spent years relaxing in plush night-club chairs were transferred to traffic, and quit.

Soon the original four hundred had been trimmed in half and were replaced by war veterans. Even more important, the royal family of fifty police captains had been cut down to fifteen, most of them new faces.

The overhauled police force then got orders to clean up and close up. The bookies who operated wide open all around City Hall got their walking papers. So did the rest of the tenderloin, which complained loudly and bitterly that this young punk was draining the city of its glamour. But Morrison wasn't changing the good food and the scenery; he was just getting rid of some of the syphilis and crime.

In a referendum, the people had backed Chep seven to one on his proposal to legalize gambling, but the state legislature had turned thumbs down. Chep was just trying to do what Mayor Shakespeare had done back in 1815: recognize that people gambled, and tax and control it, thereby giving the city a lot of money for things like hospitals and playgrounds. But when that plan was vetoed, he had to put the gamblers out of business "because gambling means payoffs and payoffs mess up a city administration something awful."

The "weed watchers" went, too. They were a lot of Maestri deadheads on the city payroll, paid to walk around and watch weeds. Under civil service, the mayor had to show cause before firing personnel, but the graft was easy to dig up and Chep bluffed out a lot of others. It added up to a thousand salaries.

Part of that found money went into salary increases. More of it went into the Department of Recreation for parks, the newly created Bureau of Juvenile Delinquency, and the Public Health Training Center. It also went for more efficient garbage disposal, a brand-new Veterans Department and another one called Latin American Affairs.

That was sort of a small-scale state department to drum up trade and good will with the Americas. Morrison was much criticized for his three trips to thirteen Latin American countries. But it all fits in with Chep's plan to boom trade for his city, which is already second only to New York as a U. S. shipping point for world trade. Besides planning a new four-hundred-million-dollar tidewater canal to double the hundred ship berths, he's been busy getting more and more air traffic to run through New Orleans. Officially, Chep has already changed the city's motto from "The City That Care Forgot" to "Air Hub of the Americas."

If Chep has any bright ideas of a political future, and he probably has, he's keeping his mouth shut about it. The only thing he'll say is that he wants to be as good a mayor as LaGuardia was. But his close friends say other things. They say that Chep can follow Sam Jones all the way up. Jones will probably run for governor in '48, or else take on Ellender in the race for the U. S. Senate. Passage of the bond issue has brightened the whole political picture for the Independents.

Now that Chep has the money to do what he wants, Louisiana politicians say that Chep's biggest problem is himself.

"Chep is still a colonel in a lot of ways. Too cocky, a little conceited, and snobbish. He needs to get his ears pinned back a few times. But when that's done, he'll do a fine job. He's a good boy."

For the fourteen Joes of Section 1, Battery D, 548th AAA, parked somewhere in the middle of nowhere—for them, their daily bull session is their whole life.

It always starts out by razzing somebody. They'll razz Short-stop because a barmaid in Chicago wouldn't give him a double Scotch that he ordered because she thought he was too young —so she gave him a small root beer instead; they'll razz "Brooklyn" for the night he thought he saw a German para-trooper and it turned out to be a helmet liner on a fence post; they'll razz Hank because he never says anything but always has a smile on his face; and they'll razz Kirkovich because he's the only "cherry" in the section.

Then whenever there's a lull in the conversation, some-body will pop out of the quiet with:

"And what's so hot about Texas?" For hours after that, the two Texans in the outfit will tell all over again about the size, production, independence, beautiful women, and cattle of Texas.

And that's the way it goes night after night. When the talk is done, somebody will stick his head out of the hole and say that maybe tomorrow will be a nice day, maybe we'll get some new magazines, maybe we'll get some visitors, maybe we'll see some planes to shoot at.

Comes dawn, they'll all pile out of their holes, rain or shine, strip and clean the guns and somebody will say:

"And what's so hot about Tennessee?" Then the day will have begun.

29

BATTLE IN TENNESSEE

"*We have chicken stealers and hog stealers! Horse stealers and auto stealers! But the lowest, dirtiest of all are election stealers. . . .*"

"*To the GI Patriots, Athens, Tenn.:*

"*Thank you indeed for restoring the faith in America which so many of us had lost. Keep pitching and firing when necessary. . . .*"

"*YOU CHOSE THE EVIL WAY. . . .*"

"*We don't expect any bullets to fly up here in Brooklyn, but the political machine here is a tight-fisted organization in full control of everything, and we will only win if all the veterans turn out and give us a hand. . . .*"

"*I congratulate you in memory of my son who lies buried in the South Pacific. . . .*"

"*We have returned from the war to find our home-grown Hitlers . . . most of us didn't care . . . a few of us griped and let it go at that . . . you and your friends are apparently the first ones who had the guts to do something about it. . . .*"

It was Saturday afternoon and the streets were lined thick with parked cars, the folks waiting to get into the two theatres, the kids filling up the fountain chairs at the four drug stores. At the Southern Soda Shop, next to the post office, the teenagers hushed when you mentioned the Battle of Athens. Then a blond-headed boy said in an offhand, exaggerated tone, "Oh, it was just a minor affair. . . ." Two of the girls giggled.

"The papers gave us such a bad reputation," said Betty Ann Johnson, her cute face screwed up seriously. "They all thought it was awful, but the people here understood. Besides, it was wonderful the way it turned out—nobody got killed."

"I got in one shot with a gun," said a youngster in a green wool shirt and a high-pitched voice.

"There's one thing I still can't get used to," added smiling Billy Cook. "All the policemen here used to be so old and fat. Now they're young and skinny."

No, they hadn't yet discussed it in their classes. They didn't know why. Sure, they'd probably discuss it someday. . . .

A block away was the town square. All the main streets clustered around the old McMinn County courthouse, with the big clock in its lantern tower and the green lawn and the maple trees and the benches filled with quiet-talking people. This was the heart of the Tennessee Bible belt, lying in the lush Sweetwater Valley, almost in the foothills of the Great Smokies. From here, people commuted to work at Oak Ridge's atomic plant, and high school kids thought nothing of driving the fifty-seven miles to either Knoxville or Chattanooga to hear some dance band. McMinn County had 33,000 people, 11,000 of them in Athens, and, technically, none of them was supposed to drink anything stronger than beer—this was one of Tennessee's dry counties. This was also probably the only county in the country that ever independently declared war against a foreign power. That was in 1898 when McMinn passed a resolution declaring war against Spain. Two weeks later, the United States followed suit. And during the Civil War there had been a bitter fight near the county jail.

The jail was an old two-story red brick building sitting behind two huge cottonwood trees. On the porch was young Deputy Sheriff Edsel Underwood. He was only twenty-two, but you couldn't say he was too young to be a deputy—he had been a platoon sergeant with the 35th Division. Seated comfortably in an ancient cretonne-covered rocker, he talked about his town:

"It was too bad we had to use guns to clean out the political gangsters." He spoke in a soft Tennessee accent, full of feeling. "But what else could we do? The courts wouldn't help us. Neither would the governor or the F.B.I.—nobody. We had to do it ourselves."

He pointed across the street to a small white house up behind some high hedges. "See that window on the right? That's where I was shooting from."

The thing that griped him, he said, was the way a lot of folks were already complaining. From the way some people talked, they expected new roads and schools to be built the day after the veterans were elected. Not only that, he added, but they were all so busy patching their political fences that they were forgetting all about this non-partisan cooperation.

"Why don't you go over to the courthouse tonight? They're having a Good Government League meeting. . . ."

The tired men in the half-filled room listened quietly to their greying, quick-talking president, L. H. Dooley, tell them all the things the League had done so far. Committees were busy investigating county expenses, the bad situation in schools and roads, the need for a more equitable tax reassessment. When he finished, the questions came slowly, and only from a few. There was only a small sprinkling of young men in the room and two of the older ones in the back row seemed to be snoozing. Even after the young University of

Tennessee professor spoke vigorously about a county manager plan, there was still this heavy apathy.

"If you could only have seen this room the day after the battle," said young John Peck, the newly-elected representative to the state legislature. "If you could have heard the way everybody got up and talked their hearts out about their faith in the democracy they had fought for. The room was so packed, you couldn't even squeeze in. One guy got up and yelled, 'Now that the crooks are gone, let's have some order around here. Let's be our own bosses. . . .' And they all stood up shouting, 'You can count on me. . . .' If you could have heard how they all cheered. . . ."

He looked at the slowly emptying room. "It's hard to believe that this is the same room, that these are some of the same people. . . ."

But then, only a week after the original meeting, John Peck himself had written in the *Daily Post-Athenian*:

"What happened to all those people who swarmed the town when the rumor of a new battle got started last Saturday night? Why did they go home and put up their guns and immediately forget all about the business of government? Must we always have the threat of violence to get the people aroused to the point where they will take an active part in their government?"

It was the same public apathy that had swept Paul Cantrell into power back in 1936. Cantrell, a nervous, heavy-set man with a fondness for gambling, had just returned from Kentucky. It was rumored he had gambled away his inheritance. His father had left Paul and his brothers big chunks of real estate plus the bank in near-by Etowah.

Back in McMinn County, Cantrell looked over the political situation and liked what he saw. The sheriff's job, paid on a piecework commission basis, was a good thing. All you had to do was keep the jails full, fine everybody the usual $16.05, and it added up to a lot of money.

The Republicans had been in power for a long time, so it wasn't hard for Cantrell to take over the disorganized Democrats. He borrowed considerable money from his brothers and used it for a hot campaign, at a time when votes were bought and sold like groceries. Still, it was close, everything hinging on the returns from the Twelfth Precinct. But Cantrell carried it by an overwhelming margin.

It was a little too overwhelming, and ten years later, a frustrated Cantrell follower, Clyde Rogers, told why. It had been quite simple. Rogers, then an election official in that precinct, merely invited the other officials to bring the ballot box to his home. He suggested they could all enjoy a good supper and then leisurely count the ballots afterwards. Only while they were eating, somebody opened the bedroom door and switched a carefully stuffed ballot box for the original.

"That Cantrell was smart, you got to hand it to him," remarked the Athens Legion Post Commander, C. A. Anderson. "When he was first elected, he didn't start grabbing right away; he worked slowly. First he forced through a ripper bill, re-districting our nineteen precincts into twelve. Told everybody he was streamlining it for efficiency, and lots of people believed him. But what it meant was that the nineteen justices of the peace had to resign and Cantrell could pick his own twelve to do what he told them. Anybody Cantrell's deputies brought in got fined, no matter what. I'll tell you this; the county jail is empty now for the first time in ten years."

In the months that followed, the county's small-scale bootlegging and gambling started blossoming, slowly at first, then bloomed wide open. Oaks Dinner Club and Halfway Court were two of the fancier places, but smaller ones soon sprouted all over the city. To get businessmen to back him, Cantrell started adjusting tax assessments up and down, depending on who was for or against him. He never had to worry about campaign funds.

But, soon, he didn't even have to worry much about campaigns. For deputies, he imported a lot of thugs with prison records, men like Minus Wilburn; for the State House of Representatives, Cantrell picked George Woods, fired from his truck-driving job when he was caught selling county gravel. Then Cantrell sent burly Pat Mansfield, a tough locomotive engineer from Georgia, to the State Senate. Through them, he had a firm liaison with Boss Crump in Memphis, who ruled the state.

"It was like Germany here," added thirty-seven-year-old, greying, ex-lieutenant commander Ralph Duggan. "Cantrell's deputies were nothing but a lot of swaggering, strutting storm troopers, drunk most of the time, beating up our citizens for the slightest reason. Know what they did? In elections, they just kicked out the poll watchers or else they took the ballot boxes to be counted in the privacy of Cantrell's bank. They even used guns and blackjacks back in 1940 to prevent four hundred people in Claxton from voting."

For three years lawyer Duggan pushed the Claxton case until a circuit court jury brought in a guilty verdict against three Cantrell deputies. But the judge simply fined the deputies one cent each, told them to be good boys and let them go free. The U. S. Supreme Court wouldn't rule on it, said it was a state matter. As for the State Supreme Court, everybody knew it was packed with Crump-picked men. So, legally, they were licked.

Some high-school kids, led by their class president and football star, Jim Buttram, wrote a letter in 1940 to several national picture magazines:

"*Dear Editor:*

If you want a good story about how a bunch of gangsters are running this town, come here on Election Day. . . ."

But the magazines never answered.

When war came, McMinn County contributed more than three thousand men, but, somehow, Cantrell managed to hold onto all his deputies. With the courts ruling against them, and their young men gone, the flickering opposition to Cantrell was smothered. When deputy Minus Wilburn shot and killed a Seabee at Halfway Court, Reverend Huling dared to preach against the murder. That same night the preacher's car was burned, his life threatened.

"It wasn't really a town any more," declared Jim Buttram, "it was a jail."

Buttram thought about it often. Here he was, a rifleman with the 9th Division, fighting all through Tunisia, Sicily and Normandy, getting wounded twice, fighting for a world concept of democracy, and there wasn't even any democracy in his own home town. It didn't make sense. When Buttram visited his wounded school buddy, Edgar Self, in a Paris hospital, their talk seethed with a sort of helplessness. How could they clean up this mess? What did they know about politics? Most of their friends were barely old enough to vote.

Their elders weren't doing much good either. Persuaded to run for mayor in 1945, round-faced, friendly C. A. Anderson, novelty wholesaler and Legion commander, told the scared people what they knew: how Cantrell had never opened the Veterans Service Office for which money had been appropriated, how the city part of the state road tax always disappeared, how Cantrell had never let the city police make a single arrest in nine years, and much, much more. . . .

His words were wasted on the wind. The whole town knew

before election day that Anderson would lose by a seven-to-one margin—the tally sheets had already been made out.

When it was all over, Cantrell raised the tax assessment on Anderson's property an additional thousand dollars.

The GI's were getting discharged quickly by Spring '46, and it didn't take the McMinn veterans long to feel the town's shame and fear, to smell the rotten political stink. The high-school boys were men now: men no longer afraid of thugs with guns; men who wouldn't step aside when Cantrell's gangsters told them to; men who shoved back when they were shoved, hit back when they were hit.

One evening in C. A. Anderson's big empty home, six men talked through the night. Besides Anderson, there was Buttram, Ralph Duggan, Edgar Self, Charles Scott, Jr. The only non-vet there was Otto Kennedy, leader of the Republican opposition to Cantrell.

"It was on April 17th," smiled Self. "My wife never lets me forget that date. I was supposed to take her to the Easter Cantata. I didn't think we'd talk for more than a couple hours."

They started talking about general problems and went home with specific answers. Suppose they wait until the next election when they would be better organized? "No . . . now . . . let's do it now . . ." Should they join with the Republicans who were already politically organized? "No . . . let's do it on a non-partisan basis . . . let's take our fight to the whole people. . . ." But if they lost, they would all have to leave town. "We're not gonna lose. . . ."

Finding candidates wasn't easy, but they did. All five were combat veterans without any previous political record. The problem was to sell these candidates to the other veterans in the county before their first mass meeting on June 9.

"That's the only criticism we got about the whole thing,"

continued Buttram, "the fact that a few of us hand-picked the candidates and sort of forced them through. But we had to. Otherwise we wouldn't have had an equal distribution of Democrats and Republicans on the ticket and it wouldn't have been non-partisan."

The turnout of four hundred angry veterans at the court-house on convention day cancelled Cantrell plans to pack the meeting and break it up. The vets then tried to pack Cantrell's own Democratic convention several weeks later. But Cantrell hired a band of gypsies, brought them to the Athens High School gym and told them how to vote.

Cantrell still would have been a shoo-in on a three-way split if the Republicans had put up their own election slate. But they didn't. They openly supported the Non-Partisan Veterans League. Cantrell had three previous terms as sheriff, two as senator. In this election he was again running for sheriff, trading jobs with Pat Mansfield.

"Did you ever read a telephone book?" asked Buttram. "Well, that's the way we raised our money. We'd read each name aloud and then figure out on whose side he was and how much we should ask him for. Then one of us would say, 'I'll take him.' What surprised us was the money we got from a lot of businessmen who had always backed Cantrell. We called it 'conscience money' because they always paid us cash instead of checks, and they always asked us, 'Please don't tell anybody . . .'"

The Non-Partisan Veterans League collected eight thousand dollars. Eight thousand for newspaper and radio advertising, for loudspeakers, for handbills thrown from Piper Cubs, for gasoline to go from precinct to precinct. Knox Henry, would-be sheriff, neglected his gas station; Frank Carmichael forgot about his Etowah farm; twenty-nine-year-old George Painter, running for county court clerk, stopped being a mechanic; Bill Hamby postponed his business plans, and World War I veteran Charlie Pickel decided he'd rather be a register of deeds than a carpenter.

For three months they went from Etowah to Englewood, Clearwater to Cog Hill, Tranquility to Mt. Harmony, Idlewild to Piney Grove, Union McMinn to Calhoun, every village schoolhouse in the county. The old-fashioned campaign of buttonholing, doorbell ringing. And, always, in every speech, every handbill, every radio program, they repeated over and over again, "YOUR VOTE WILL BE COUNTED AS CAST."

It had a catchy sound of hope, and the people heard it so often that soon they were saying among themselves, "Well . . . maybe . . ."

The campaign took on its sizzling heat in the middle of July, several weeks before election. Until then, Cantrell had done almost no campaigning. It wasn't campaigns, it was vote-counting that won elections, and he planned to take care of that as usual.

But then the veterans started their fifteen-minute radio program over the Athens station, WLAR, and they didn't bother with fuzzy political double talk—they asked direct questions. Who sold the county road machinery? What about the murder of the Seabee? And what about the Cantrell storm troopers, the rake-offs from bootlegging and gambling, the stealing of poll tax receipts from our veterans while they're beaten in jail?

They hammered like that every day and the town buzzed with it. At first Cantrell tried to laugh it off, then got annoyed. Finally he got mad enough to make his first big mistake. He hired radio time to answer the charges. He denied everything, even the most obvious corruption.

"The charge of open gambling and selling whiskey over

the bar is absolutely false; the allegation that GI's have been arrested and their poll tax receipts taken away from them does not contain a word of truth . . . for the past ten years McMinn County elections have been cleaner than they have been in the history of the county. . . ."

The whole town listened. To them it was funnier than Fibber McGee. Who did he think he was kidding? For hours after each Cantrell broadcast, the party lines were full of the laughter of the town.

With their laughter, came more hope:

"You know what, Tom, these boys may do it. Did you hear about how they cut down Cantrell's list of absentee voters from 1200 to 400? They just cut out the names of all those people who were dead and buried. These boys are mad, and they're not scared. Maybe. . . ."

News also spread about the letter Jim Buttram got from George Woods, Cantrell's election commissioner, who was also county purchasing agent, budget clerk, and Boss Crump's speaker of the lower house of the state legislature. Woods wrote:

"Dear Jim:

I've known you and your father for a long time now. You don't really think I'd steal an election, do you?"

And Buttram had answered, "You better not. . . ."

About that time people also heard what Cantrell's deputies did to Charley Parris. They brought him to City Hall and forced him to sign a statement denying that his poll tax receipt was taken away from him while he was in jail. Charley signed, but told all about it afterwards.

There were more people at the Non-Partisan rallies now and there was a different spirit about them. Instead of coming out of curiosity, they came with faith. And when a speaker

said, "Your vote will be counted as cast," they didn't applaud
—they cheered.

Still, there were plenty of skeptics around, people who said,
"Yeah, those are nice words, 'counted as cast,' but how you
gonna do it?"

Their Congressman Jennings had presented a thousand
affidavits to the Department of Justice testifying to Cantrell's
crookedness in past elections. A dozen different appeals had
been made to the state Attorney General, the F.B.I. in Knoxville, the Governor, asking them to send men to supervise a
fair election. But nobody was interested.

So they turned to the people. On the radio, the ex-GI's
said, "Come to the election next Thursday and bring your
flashlights. We have an excellent power system, but our lights
have a peculiar habit of going out while our votes are being
counted. Also, bring your lunch, stay all day and far into the
night so you can see that your vote is counted as cast."

But when they broadcast this message to the people, the
veterans had their fingers crossed. Because nobody, even then,
knew exactly what the people would do on August 1. Nobody
knew how many would really vote and how many would stay
to watch their votes counted. Even at their high pitch of
optimism, there was still a basic fear buried deep in the people.
The most persistent rumor still was that Cantrell would "get"
anybody who openly opposed him.

The day before election, in his daily front-page column,
"An Editor Comments on the Friendly City of Progressive
East Tennessee," Lowell Arterburn wrote, "Both factions
have indicated that a fair election will be held." The next
midnight Arterburn confessed he had almost dropped the
words "Friendly City" from his column title. "We are prepared to bow our heads in shame with the citizens of Mc-

Minn County . . . this is a terrible thing that we have experienced. . . ."

The "terrible thing" started early that morning. While long lines of people waited to vote outside the Third Precinct polling place in Etowah, an ex-GI election watcher named Evans said to the election judge, "I'd like to look inside that ballot box first, if you don't mind."

The judge smiled, "Oh you would, would you?"

Two minutes later several deputies dragged a badly beaten Evans to jail. The judge appointed a Cantrell man to take his place.

But the real trouble started that afternoon on Athens' North Jackson Street. Tom Gillespie came to vote at the Eleventh Precinct in the Water Works Building, the same place he had been voting for years. Cantrell Deputy Windy Wise held Gillespie's thin ballot to the light, saw whom he was voting for, and said, "Get the hell out of here. . . ." When old Gillespie protested, Windy slugged him with his brass knuckles. Gillespie staggered, started running, and Windy yelled to the other deputies, "Grab that nigger . . ." Then he pulled out his gun and shot Gillespie in the back.

Shortly afterwards, at the same polling place, Mrs. Vestal and a group of parents and teachers told election judge Karl Neil that they wanted to stay to watch the ballot-counting. Mrs. Vestal's son Ed had to stand still and listen to Neil tell his mother to get out and stay out—there was a gun sticking in Ed's back.

Later, though, gun or no gun, Vestal and Charles Scott, Jr., both objected when Karl Neil placed two deputies so as to hide the ballot box. Neil just laughed at them.

Suddenly, there was a crash of breaking glass, and women screamed. A crowd of several hundred people tensed while they watched Scott and Vestal stumbling forward in the street, their faces covered with blood.

"Let's go get 'em," a man yelled.

Instinctively, the crowd surged forward, curving to absorb Scott and Vestal, pushing toward the broken glass window. But fifteen deputies quickly formed a semicircle in front of the building, pointing their guns at the crowd to keep them back.

"Oh my God, here it comes," a woman screeched.

Within minutes, the ballot box had been dumped into one of the waiting cars. The deputies then piled in, and the cars drove back to the jail, leaving behind a noisy, confused crowd.

Almost at the same time, in a restaurant in the Twelfth Precinct on North White Street, election watcher Bill Hairell asked a young girl how old she was.

"I'm seventeen."

"Well you're underage, you can't vote . . ."

Deputy Minus Wilburn scowled, "Hell, she can't." When they carried Bill to jail, his skull had been split wide open by Wilburn's blackjack and his face was all bloodied from where it had been kicked.

It was a different street scene on West Washington Street in front of the EssandKay Tire Company garage, where the Kennedy boys had beaten three insulting deputies while a big crowd watched, cheered and jeered:

"You boys ain't so tough once you lose your guns. . . ."

Four more deputies wandered by and the three Kennedy boys grabbed them, too, this time some of the crowd joining in to black a few eyes, rip some clothes. The crowd cheered when the seven deputies, minus their badges, guns and pants were forced into several cars to be let out at the city limits. But there were still almost two hundred other Cantrell deputies scattered around the county.

Another sweating deputy was sitting and counting votes in the Niota schoolhouse while several hundred citizens solemnly looked on. Earlier Cantrell's deputies had tried to clear the polling place of watchers, but the people simply swarmed in and overwhelmed the deputies. Then somebody read aloud the part from State Election Code 2087 permitting any citizen to watch the ballot counting.

Elsewhere, in Athens, a citizen read aloud the section from the Declaration of Rights in the Tennessee Constitution, "that government, being instituted for the common benefit, the doctrine of non-resistance against arbitrary power and oppression is absurd, slavish, and destructive of the good and happiness of mankind."

That was the thinking that night of the big crowd of angry, loud-talking people who marched down to the jail, where they stopped and stilled while one of them shouted out of the darkness, "Bring out those ballot boxes . . ."

From inside the jail, a deputy laughed, "Why don't you call the law . . ." The answer came back quickly, cutting the laughter short, "There is no law in McMinn County."

It was a long, stretched-out silence that lasted several seconds and then a deputy yelled, "Aw, go to hell. . . ."

Just then somebody inside the jail fired at the crowd, hitting an ex-marine named Gunter in the leg. The crowd scattered. From behind a hedge across the street, somebody fired at the jail. The Battle of Athens had started at ten minutes after nine.

"C'mon get guns . . . get some guns. . . ."

They came from everywhere. Farmers with old shotguns that hadn't been fired in years, vets with .45's and rifles, kids with BB guns. Other men had broken into the armory for more arms and ammunition. A machine gun sat on top of the movie theatre overlooking the jail. Another .30 caliber was parked behind a hedge near the post office across the street.

"At first I thought it was just a lot of firecrackers going off," remembered Mrs. Wilson, who lived in the white house facing the jail. "But these boys came in with rifles and told us we better lie down on the floor. They were firing from the kitchen window and we could hear the bullets hitting the drainpipe and the plaster falling down. One bullet hit the faucet and turned on the water full force. It even scared the boys who were shooting. My four kids were all crying so I took them down to the Southern Soda Shop. Everybody there was scared too."

It was like a wild west show with the mob of people milling in the side streets, a few of them ducking the ricochets to come and get a peek now and then, racing away when the machine guns opened up. Chuck Redfern had the town's grandstand seat. Chuck was reporting the battle all night long over WLAR and the window of the radio station overlooked the whole scene. To get personal quotes, Chuck would occasionally race downstairs and talk to some of the men doing the shooting. One young vet told him, "I ain't had so much fun since Guadalcanal." An older man said, more seriously, "We're gonna have a brighter tomorrow."

Finally somebody informed Chuck, "We're gonna dynamite the jail . . . tell that over WLAR. . . ."

It was past two that morning when word of the dynamiting swept through the crowd and a woman started screaming on Gettys Street, "Don't do it . . . I've got a boy in that jail. . . ." Another woman crept behind a near-by hedge and yelled at the top of her lungs to her husband inside the jail, "Don't be a fool, Bill . . . come on out . . . you wanna get killed. . . ."

The rest of the crowd cheered at the news, except for some

old people who were praying aloud, "Our Father who art in Heaven . . ."

An ex-GI, who knew how, wiggled close and threw a single stick of dynamite, purposely short. After a long interval, with a second warning to the deputies inside, the second charge, two sticks, landed closer. The next one, three sticks, still closer and Chuck Redfern watched the blast bounce the needle off his recording machine and told the radio audience, "It won't be long now."

The concussion of the last charge broke loose the swing and rocked the building. Before the smoke cleared away, the deputies were yelling hysterically, "Okay . . . we give up . . . we're coming out. . . ."

"They were scared crazy," said one of the veterans who went into the jail with the first bunch. "They were crawling around the floor, some of them crying, some of them saying their prayers. One of them grabbed me around the knees and begged me to save him. They all thought we were going to kill them right away. . . ."

They had good reason to think so. Outside some two dozen new cars belonging to the deputies were being hacked, overturned, burned.

Cantrell, Mansfield, the two state highway patrolmen, and many of the others had managed to sneak away leaving about thirty-five deputies in the jail. When the thirty-five were marched out single file, their hands stuck high in the air, the crowd yelled,

"String 'em up . . ."

"Kill the bastards . . ."

"Turn 'em loose and let's see how fast they can run . . ."

Quickly the hysteria, the car-burning, and the mounting excitement of deep-rooted hate was turning the crowd into a mob, a mob ready to do anything.

"I want your attention. . . . I want your attention . . . listen to me. . . ."

It was Ralph Duggan, standing on top of a car, yelling as loudly as he could. Slowly the crowd quieted.

"We've won our victory . . . the votes will be counted as cast . . . there won't be any more gangster rule in Athens . . . but we're not murderers. . . . If we treat these thugs the way they treated us then we're as bad as they are . . . I ask you to go home peacefully . . . remember . . . the whole country is watching what we're doing here tonight. . . ."

The tension of tight silence broke. Slowly, reluctantly, the crowd started breaking up. But there was still a small knot of people around the much-hated Minus Wilburn and by the time Duggan got there, somebody had slashed Wilburn's neck. Duggan used finger pressure to stop him from bleeding to death.

By this time Cantrell's election commissioner, George Woods, had called from Chattanooga promising to come into Athens and sign the election certificates, if they would protect him. Frank Cantrell called soon afterwards from Etowah to concede the election for his brother Paul, who was hiding in a church basement somewhere in Athens. Meanwhile, the six tampered-with ballot boxes had been thrown out; the other six had shown the GI's elected overwhelmingly by more than two to one.

But the show wasn't over. When Reverend Bernie Hampton came to town at nine that Friday morning (his wife had kept him home the night before) he saw this huge crowd again gathered around the jail. The veterans were letting the deputies out a few at a time and the people had come to heckle. But their heckling mood had turned into something dangerously ugly. The crowd egged on one citizen who stepped up to a newly released, still-cowering deputy, socked him in the face and shouted, "That's for breaking my ribs. . . ."

Just as Duggan had done the night before, Hampton climbed up on an overturned car and yelled, "Let's not lose our heads . . . we've cleaned up a mess and we're all glad . . . let's keep our victory clean of violence . . . go home in peace. . . ." They went.

All that day the town throbbed with talk. The veterans had formed raiding parties. They went from one gambling joint to another to bust up all the slot machines and warn the bootleggers and gamblers to get out of town, but quick. When navy veteran Fred Puett saw Jim Buttram that day, he slapped him on the back and beamed, "Jim, you never were much of a student in my civics class, but you deserve an A right now. . . ."

That same afternoon, townspeople squeezed into the county courthouse to elect C. A. Anderson, Reverend Bernie Hampton, and J. P. Cartwright as their three-man commission until the election was made legal.

Tension simmered, settled, and then started all over again the next day. A Knoxville paper printed a story rumoring that Cantrell and Company were reinforcing and planning to storm back into Athens. WLAR broadcast the story and the courthouse phones rang all day long. People from all over eastern Tennessee, especially veterans, volunteered their help. Several carloads of men with guns came down from Chattanooga and by early afternoon almost two thousand men had filed into the courthouse to register their guns.

An ex-infantry captain planned the town's defense, deploying groups to set up roadblocks at strategic points along the highway, setting up supply lines, ammunition dumps, an evacuation setup for the wounded. On the rooftops of the courthouse square, seventy-five sharpshooters were settled snug, watching, waiting.

When a reporter wanted to know what a middle-aged woman was doing with a rifle in the arcade of the Robert E. Lee Hotel, she answered grimly, "I've got a husband and a son in this Athens citizen army and I'm ready to join them if they need me. . . ."

But they didn't. For all the tension, it was just a quiet Saturday night. Only nobody thought anything of a young man walking down the street with a girl on one arm and a gun on the other. A photographer taking a picture of an armed youngster in a jalopy, quoted him as saying, "Heck, I missed all the fun Thursday night and I thought I'd get a chance to fire this thing at least once today. . . ."

Sunday morning was even quieter. It was a warm clear day and the men had put away their guns and were pushing baby carriages. And when people went to church that morning, they walked right by the jail, instead of detouring like they usually did. The next day the paper commented, "The people went to church thankful that the gangsters had gone, thankful that nobody had been killed, thankful that the voice of the people could again be heard. . . ."

They could smile now when it was suggested the town's name be changed to "Fort Athens." And wasn't it funny about the mayor's secretary never notifying him because she didn't want to spoil his South Carolina vacation? And the Governor, who wouldn't help them before, now promising everybody a complete investigation, how do you like that?

But the biggest joke of all concerned ex-sheriff Pat Mansfield. He had quickly moved back to Cartersville, Georgia, where he told the local editor: "Why, I could have killed dozens of my fellow citizens, but the very thought of such a thing was so revolting that I would not fire myself nor would I permit my deputies to do so. . . ."

This was no small local thing that had happened. Within a week, the people of McMinn, with considerable surprise, discovered how their revolt had captured the imagination of the country. Some editorial writers referred to it in terms of the Boston Tea Party, others condemned it as dangerously fascist. But nowhere was the whole story printed. From everywhere came clippings and columns and headlines and letters: *New York Times*, Jehovah's Witnesses, Eleanor Roosevelt, a furniture store owner in Kosciusko, Woman's Christian Temperance Union, a GI in Japan, a professor of tropical horticulture in Hawaii.

There was an urgent wire from Washington: "Me and my outfit prays most humbly to associate ourselves with you. If acceptable, wire instructions collect. Our dope is infinite, tangible and inflammable, if not to say, explosive . . ."; a Harvard student asked permission to come down and write a thesis about what had happened; an old man wanted to sell them a detailed plan for a new type of government for only five hundred dollars, "so I can build me a shanty to live in for the rest of my life"; somebody from the Bronx wired, "We must act quickly to form a new veterans' party—North, South, East, and West . . ."; a retired schoolteacher wrote:

"Dear GI's: will you now be kind enough to see what you can do about increasing our pensions?"; mothers of dead soldiers sent money and prayers, old men sent advice, politicians sent feelers, veterans all over the country wrote, "Can you please come and help us clean up our local political mess. . . ."

Jim Buttram got most of the mail, a big boxful of it, including one from an old school friend who wrote: "I always knew you were very capable from the time you outmanaged me and eleven others in the McMinn High School Beauty Contest." There was also one which said, "I'm a sixty-seven-year-old non-vet who has never voted but I love fair play and I *like* men with GUTS to get it. . . ." Another man asked him to please help him find his brother who had escaped from a mental institution, and finally, there was a short note which said: "The Athens Garden Club wants you to know it has voted approval of what you have done. . . ."

Meanwhile McMinn County quickly relaxed back to normal. The local VFW post held a victory dance featuring hula-hula girls, the Etowah High School Class of '40 had their steak barbecue reunion on schedule, and the new sheriff had the jail repapered and repainted until it looked like new. Only the milkman complained: the sudden emigration of Cantrell followers from the town had cost him a lot of business.

But if the political fever was dying in McMinn, it had been caught up and was flaming elsewhere. Non-partisan veterans organizations sprouted all over Tennessee, spreading quickly all over the South. In Tennessee's Polk County, bossed by Burch Biggs, Crump's Number Two man, fear of another Athens battle kept the election clean—and the vets won. The healthiest sign of all was in Chattanooga, where the veterans and non-vets combined to sponsor a non-vet for top office.

The fever spread widely enough so that Jim Buttram was approached to head a state non-partisan veterans group, and call a convention of representatives from each county. But Buttram, old for his twenty-four years, first wanted each representative double-checked to make sure he really represented a non-partisan group, instead of a front for some political faction wanting control. That stalled it.

Things like that worry Buttram seriously. He's been afraid that the Athens revolt would set off a chain reaction of violence, or set a pattern for future veteran action all around the country.

Specifically there was this veterans group in Asheville, North Carolina, which wanted Buttram to come down and spark their convention to a little more action. First, Buttram investigated. The vet leaders there were just a bunch of bums with no legitimate gripe. Buttram's afraid that there are plenty of similar bums who could easily be persuaded to serve as fronts for all kinds of fascist hate groups.

As for McMinn County itself, old-time state politicians label the whole non-partisan movement as a temporary phase. They point to the fact that attendance at Good Government League meetings has been dropping off, that the whole history of reform movements in this country has shown that original enthusiasms dampen quickly. Then it becomes politics as usual, with the people again letting politicians run things. The next McMinn election would unquestionably be Democrats vs. Republicans, they say.

But they all agreed this much was sure: Cantrell and Co. were through in McMinn and there would be no more election-stealing for a long, long time.

Maybe it was partly because a guy like Jim Buttram, who helped his dad in the grocery market, would always carry a much-folded piece of paper in his wallet. Datelined Fifth Service Command Separation Center, Buttram had underlined these words, "If you see intolerance and hate, speak out against them . . . make your individual voices heard, not for selfish things, but for honor and decency among men, for the rights of all people. Remember, too, that *no* American can afford to be disinterested in any part of his government whether it is county, city, state or nation. . . ."

Just a few days before, they had been laughing and singing in the streets, waving flags, bringing out their best wine, racing alongside our jeeps so that they could touch our hands or get a smile. Only a few stayed inside behind closed shutters. But everybody knew then who was on whose side.

Now the happy, laughing ones were crowded in close clusters on the street corners, staring intently at all military traffic, considering carefully how many trucks were empty, how many were full, which way they were going.

The news had spread fast: "The Americans are leaving. . . . The Germans are coming back. . . ."

Those to whom this meant death were already on the road, whole families piled onto sagging horsecarts, sometimes riding, sometimes walking, women, children, old people.

And jeering at them, spitting at them, walking down the streets laughing and happy and singing were the handful who stayed indoors behind shutters when the Americans had come.

30

FIGHT IT WHERE YOU FIND IT

IF YOU'VE never heard of Hodding Carter, you will. He's a dark-haired man about forty, only he looks younger, and he happens to be the conscience of a town called Greenville, Mississippi.

Greenville is in the heart of the rich delta country, and its twenty thousand citizens pride themselves on being more tolerant than the hill-folks. And they are. If Hodding Carter tried to publish his *Delta Times-Democrat* up in the hill country, he might be getting himself shot at by now.

Because Hodding Carter, winner of a Pulitzer prize, a Nieman award, a Guggenheim fellowship, and honorary degrees from Bowdoin and Harvard, is what a lot of good Greenville citizens call "a nigger lover."

They can't call him a damyankee, because he was born and raised in the South. So some people say he's "a furriner from Louisiana who spends his summer vacations up in Maine." Others call him a Red, even though they know he isn't. It's just a tag pinned onto anybody who's even slightly suspected of trying to overturn the racial apple cart.

A Greenville grocer had this to say:

"Now I like Hodding personally, you understand. But where me and him disagree is that he wants higher education for the niggers and I say no. You give them higher education and then they'll all want to know why they haven't got social equality. From the beginning of time, we've always had two classes of people: the ones who dig ditches and the ones who tell them how. Now if you give higher education to all of them, you won't have anybody left to dig ditches.

"Nobody wants to run Hodding out of town, you understand, but he's not doing Greenville any good. Maybe he's too big for this town."

What the grocer meant, and soon explained, was that Negroes outnumbered the Delta Whites three to one, and the whites were scared. They were scared of the someday when Greenville Negroes might be equally educated, first-class voting citizens. And this fear kept a high pressure on their prejudices.

That's why it takes guts to be a Hodding Carter in Greenville, to say the things he says. And all he says, is this:

The Negro is a human being. Let's give him decent housing, better educational facilities, equal pay for equal work, improved health standards.

That's all. Nothing about abolishing segregation. That's something Hodding doesn't expect to see either in his lifetime or in the lifetime of his three sons.

And yet, once upon a time, Hodding was proud of the fact that he had never even brushed his teeth in a Bowdoin College lavatory because a Negro student had used it.

There was no specific thing that changed his thinking. It was a slow change, stretched out over years of questioning. The questioning started at Columbia School of Journalism, continued at Tulane University where he taught for a year, and went on while he was with the *New Orleans Item*, which paid him twelve dollars a week to write simple, hard facts.

He married a fine-featured girl named Betty who had

similar questions about their South. The big question was: How far do we want to go?

It took a long time before they found an answer to that one. Meanwhile they invested all of $367 to buy a newspaper in Hammond, Louisiana, Hodding's home town. They traded advertising for office space and food, learned how to repair a rickety seventy-five-dollar printing press and somehow scrounged enough dollar bills every week to meet their small payroll.

Those were the days when Huey Long was the undisputed dictator of Louisiana. Yet here was a twenty-six-year-old nobody named Hodding Carter, editing a run-down paper, writing blasting editorials against the Louisiana Kingfish. Ordinarily it wouldn't have added up to anything. But the local congressman died. And instead of letting the people pick their own candidate, Huey picked his own man, declared him the sole candidate.

That started it. People who had shut up for too long, now rallied around their voice, held meetings, organized. One night before the phony election, a crowd broke into the courthouse, burned the ballots.

When Huey ordered out the militia, the people got their guns, and there was some shooting. Afterwards they held a rump election, and sent their own candidate to contest Huey's appointment to the congressional seat. Congress seated neither, ordered another election. With the whole country watching, this one had to be honest, so Huey poured in money, propaganda, and put up his strongest candidate. He still lost.

The Hodding Carters changed their address in 1936, after Long was killed. They sold their paper at a fat profit and bought another paper in Greenville, Mississippi. Here there was a different fight waiting for them, here were the answers to their questions.

Their fight against Huey Long had been on the sharp, clear issue of corruption. Their fight against Mississippi's Rankins and Bilboes was shaded with the undertones and overtones of race hate.

The day after the brutal Duck Hill blowtorch lynching, one of Hodding's friends called to complain because there was no editorial about it.

"But Will, you haven't looked on the front page . . ."

Still, it was easy to denounce a lynching. It wasn't so easy to analyze the "why" behind it. In his first novel, *Winds of Fear*, Hodding wrote: "Racism isn't peculiar to the South. They lynch up North, and a damn sight more than we do." But then Hodding went on to stress that the lynch-minded Southerners were almost always the economically-squeezed poor whites.

But this is what a prominent lawyer in Greenville thought: "When a nigger rapes a white woman there's only one thing you can do—kill him. You just can't wait for the law."

The townspeople grumbled about Hodding's racial editorials, but nobody did anything. Then one day the whole town exploded. Phone calls, letters to the editor, telegrams, hundreds of subscription cancellations.

"What the hell do you think you're doing anyway, running a picture of a Nigra on the front page?"

It was a picture of Jesse Owens, famous track star who was attending the seventy-fifth anniversary of a near-by all-Negro town, Mound Bayou. That night Hodding wrote an editorial entitled, "The Jesse Owens Picture." It was simple. It asked why should Southern newspapers only write stories and print pictures of Negroes when they do bad things, why not give them credit for the good things they do?

The cancellations stopped coming.

These were the days when events rushed into each other. A Nieman fellowship at Harvard, a short stretch on *PM* as press editor, the war.

After bouncing around in different army jobs and co-authoring a book on civilian defense, Hodding was shipped to Cairo to put out Middle East editions of the *Stars and Stripes* and *Yank*. They finally discharged him when an infection cost him the sight of his right eye.

The first thing he saw when he came home to Greenville was a huge sign at the foot of Main Street, just where it turns off to the levee. Decorated with American flags, this gaudy red-white-and-blue sign was the town's honor roll of boys who had fought in the war. Only it was blank, it had been blank for months.

Hodding soon found out why. The Lions Club had collected dimes and dollars from the whole town to build the sign. But then they got a warning: if they dared to put the names of Negroes on that sign, it would be dynamited. Since there was no list of contributors, no money could be returned. So everything simply stopped. And there it stood, staring at the town.

Hodding wrote:

"How in God's name can the Negroes be encouraged to be good citizens, to feel that they can get a fair break . . . if we deny them so small a thing as joint service recognition. . . . This newspaper cannot force the completion of the Honor Roll. But we do say, either complete or tear it down. Today it is a stench in the nostrils of the fair-minded—who, we hopefully believe, are in the majority in Greenville as in the rest of the South."

But the sign stayed there.

When Theodore Bilbo ran for re-election, he stumped the state and screeched about the "nigger-loving" editorials of Hodding Carter and threatened to organize a skinning party to ride Hodding out of town on a rail. Hodding wrote an editorial about that:

"Theodore Bilbo's mind is so soaked in the poisonous slime of his bigotry that it reminds us of nothing so much as a neglected cesspool. That being so, we have no way of knowing what thoughts bubble beneath. But we can make a few guesses. He will probably let all of you in on the secret that we're a Communistic, Negro-loving so-and-so, who has been run out of Louisiana and Mississippi, and who is conspiring with the newspaper PM, the American press in general, the Soviet High Command and your cook to so degenerate the nation and the race that maybe our grandchildren will all be like Bilbo."

That was only the beginning. Subtle as a sledge hammer, Hodding itemized all the dirty skeletons in the Bilbo closet, and there were plenty. He even told about the time Bilbo was found in a barn hiding behind a heifer calf when he was wanted as a witness in the seduction trial of Governor Russell. A reporter had written: "Some people feel sorry for Governor Russell, others for the girl, and some even for Bilbo; but I, personally, feel sorry for the heifer calf."

But when the votes were counted, Bilbo had still carried Greenville.

"Why, we had to vote Bilbo," commented a local business-man. "The best Christian people in this town told us that. Sure he had some crackpot ideas, but it seems he's the only one in Congress who stood up for the South. I tell you a lot of people were sure mad at Hodding for what he said against Bilbo.

"Hodding don't realize it, but you gotta watch those niggers. Now take this colored woman who came in the other day. I asked her a question and she said, 'Um.' I told her right then and there that the next time she comes into my store, she better say, 'yes, sir.' After all, there's a limit to kindness. You gotta watch them or they step all over you."

Hodding has an answer for that. It's something he's been talking about to groups all over the South for years now: the fact that it isn't a question of so-called kindness, it's a question of democracy. And that if we want to sell our democracy to the world, we've got to remember that the majority of the world's people are colored, not white.

While the race issue is the hot one on his editorial page, Hodding still writes 950 out of 1,000 editorials a year which concern themselves with other things.

Because Greenville isn't just the place where Hodding Carter publishes a newspaper; it's his home. He concerns himself with everything about it. The constant fight for more schools, more playgrounds, better pay for teachers, a mobile X-ray unit, improved airport facilities, educational drives on syphilis, free lunch for school children, a TB preventorium, collections for burned-out farmers, Christmas toys for poor kids. "We're the damndest collection agency you ever saw."

When the mayor decided to fire the judge and take over his job—and salary, Hodding was first to get up and yell. And when county officials refused to pay its share of expenses to get Public Health Service to spray the malarial mosquito paradise on near-by Archer Island, Hodding scared them into coming across with the money. He warned that new industry would be discouraged from coming into a malarial area.

Besides this, Hodding has greatly expanded his paper, putting in a farm page and the first book review page in Mississippi (he printed a review of Bilbo's recent book under the title,

"Best Smeller"). In addition, Hodding has applied for an FM radio station license. And he financed his ex-managing editor, Jimmy Alsop, who set up his own paper in Greenwood, 50 miles away. Twenty-nine year old Alsop, back from Bougainville with a Purple Heart, went to work with two other veterans, Charles Pou and Frank Smith. Their first big story exposed the brutal flogging-murder of a Negro.

Hodding doesn't have to do all this. He has enough money now to quit any time, relax in the sun for the rest of his life like the doctor ordered. But, like William Allen White, he feels he has a job to do in his home town. Some of his friends have told him how they've moved away from certain places because they were too filled with prejudices. Hodding believes you have to fight prejudice where you find it.

"You don't have to be brave to be a liberal down here any more," he always says, but it isn't true. It isn't easy, living and working in a small town when you know how many people there hate you for what you believe.

"Sure a lot of people hate Hodding, a lot of them got real excited about Hodding during the Bilbo campaign. But they're calming down now. They'll be all right unless he stirs them up again."

He will.

The waves slapping and banging and the LCVP floating around in circles for two hours before H-hour and everybody sits with a helmet between his knees puking his guts out, so sick that he doesn't care what happens to him. But suddenly, the boat starts moving in and somehow you stand up and swallow what you've got in your mouth and forget you're sick.

"I took five steps," said the medic, "and this 88 lands about thirty feet to my left. Then I run to the right and bang, another 88, and this time my buddy is staring at his hand because his thumb is shot off. Then two more, just like that, and I found some backbone and ribs and the back of a skull with the whole face cleaned out, all of it right near the pack next to me."

His first patient was a guy who had his front tooth knocked out by a piece of shrapnel. His second was in a foxhole, buried up to his thighs.

"I didn't even notice it at first but he had blood spurting from his chest. Two big holes. You can't plug up a guy's lungs, brother. We did all we could though. I spotted this bottle of blood plasma that we were giving some other guy and then I noticed this other one was dead, so I just took out the needle and put it in this guy's arm. But it didn't do much good. He died in my arms."

31

4-F IN THE AMERICAN CAMPAIGN

"What did you do in the war, Daddy?" When his two little girls grew up and asked that, what would he tell them? Would he tell them that he was a 4-F, that he didn't do a damn thing? That wasn't true. He had taught five thousand soldiers in the Army Student Training Program, taught them to think, to read, to write intelligently.

Would he tell them that he didn't want to fight, that he didn't believe in war, that he was able to do more good in civilian life. Half-truths. He didn't want to die, but then who did? Still, he had tried to enlist, but they all turned him down. Army, Navy, Marines, even the F.B.I.

He didn't believe in war but he wanted to fight for democracy against fascism. But that company-owned home town of his, he wouldn't fight for that. He wouldn't fight for that big sign back home, "A gathering of three or more people constitutes a violation of the law." If he fought and died it would be for the simple words in the Bill of Rights.

Deep down, if he was honest with himself, he knew there were other reasons for wanting to enlist. Hidden personal reasons that nobody ever talked much about. The sense of belonging, the feeling of envy, the fear of being called a slacker (nobody ever did), the practical thinking about the postwar veterans' gravy train. Even more than all that, for him, there was the basic wish to be part of the Army, part of war so that he could better understand his own generation. How much of American literature wouldn't he understand because he was never in a Pacific campaign, never marched through the Italian mud, never saw somebody's head get blown off?

But then, how many had? How many of his five thousand soldier-students ever saw and felt the war, actually did the fighting and dying? Not many, he knew that. Most troops were in rear echelons, lots of them in safe soft setups. So many of his veteran friends had told him: "A helluva lot of guys never had it so good."

Well, the things he had done during the war, wasn't that as important as some clerk's job in a QM depot? Maybe he could tell his children that much.

There were other things he wouldn't tell them, not until they were much older. About his brother and close friends who had died; about the bitterness of the ones who didn't. Bitterness of thinking that all that regimentation and all that time and all those lives were for nothing if people hadn't yet learned the waste and utter stupidity of war. The question he had heard a thousand times, "It's only two years. How can they forget so quickly? How can the people talk of another war?"

Here was something he could fight without any hidden reservations—the fight against war talk, the fight for a united democratic world. As long as he could teach and preach, he would have no fear of being called a slacker in this fight. As for the feeling of belonging, he would have it in the fullest sense. How can you be more a part of the world than when you are dedicating your life to fighting for all of it?

THE tiny Congregational church in Mission Hill, South Dakota, was filled with whispering people. Whispering about the twenty-eight-year-old preacher who was going to give his first sermon that morning. Man named Robert Brigham who taught English at near-by Yankton College. Seemed like a smart, serious young man. Wonder what he'd say?

They hushed when he stepped up into the pulpit, announced his sermon, "The Dignity of Man":

"We are all guardians of each other's dignity. . . . If you deprive my brother of rights, you so deprive me . . . If my neighbor has no running water and no electricity, it affects me as much as if he has the measles. People are economically, socially, hygienically, politically, religiously interrelated. . . ."

What kind of minister was this anyway?

"If we want the world to be democratic, then we've got to preach and practice more democracy instead of hypocrisy. . . . In America and in our schools, ideas are duds. They fizzle and go out in the vast, unventilated dampness of our minds. . . ."

Who ever heard of such a thing? Their other preacher used to talk so flowery and poetic. This man's talk was so hard and real. Did it belong in a church?

But, for the next several week-ends, Robert Brigham, his wife, and their two children visited the parish members. They talked about crops and children and chitchat, and the parish liked them. Such a nice couple, the people thought, and weren't those two children just the cutest things? And, always, the people had something for the new preacher: a side of bacon, a big bag of vegetables, a dressed chicken in a shoebox.

Soon there were funerals, marriages, baptisms. The Brighams became part of Mission Hill.

Then, one day, the townspeople picked up their newspaper which had been running vicious ads against the T.V.A. and M.V.A. On the editorial page was a letter to the editor:

"My ancestors came to America in 1630. I am a Minister

in the Congregational Church. I don't think that the M.V.A. plan is either Communistic or undemocratic."

Mission Hill's party line was busy all day long. "Did you see the preacher's letter in the paper . . . what do you think?"

Brigham soon gave them even more to think about. At the Ladies Aid Society, he talked about prejudice: "You're prejudiced for one reason only: you don't know." At the Kiwanis, on the Negro problem: "Any man is as good as he proves to be, regardless of anything else."

And one Sunday the preacher walked into the pulpit with a copy of the *New Republic's* "Election Supplement" and began, "How do you think a good Christian feels about the F.E.P.C., the minimum wage bill, and the need for decent housing? Do you know whether your congressman has voted like a good Christian? Well, here's the record . . ."

Days later a political canvasser came to get Mrs. Charles Johnson's signature on a petition. Mrs. Charles Johnson who had always lived in a world of farm chores and recipe exchanges. She bristled and harumphed, "I will not sign that petition. Don't you think I know how he voted against the O.P.A.?"

When Bob Brigham reactivated the Boy Scouts, the youngsters told him how their fathers were writing letters to their congressmen for the first time; when Mary scrubbed the church floors with the other parish women and they talked about strikes, blind blaming of labor gave way to some intelligent evaluation.

This was only week-ends. Five days a week Brigham taught at Yankton College.

"I've always been able to classify my teachers," remarked one of his students, "but I can't figure out this Brigham. All I know is that he's terrific. Can you imagine a teacher in Freshman English actually trying to make his students think?"

After a banker's son got up and made a hate-speech about the CIO, Brigham persuaded him to read all about the CIO and write a term paper on it. Instead of writing about their favorite hobbies, other students were investigating the National Association of Manufacturers, the Ku Klux Klan, Republican party propaganda. Always there was free discussion, with Brigham constantly prodding, "Now what do we actually know about these things . . . what are the facts?"

It was after class that they came to him for direction—confused country kids who wanted a purpose in life. They would be social workers, reform politicians, muckrakers, so many of them wondered if they could be teachers like him.

This was Robert Irving Brigham's philosophy of education: that, fundamentally, teaching should be an awakening process; should give students an awareness of the world they live in rather than a mastery of punctuation and the pluperfect tense.

Robert Irving Brigham, A.B., B.S., M.A., M.Ed., Ph.D in Education, another Ph.D in English—this was a different Brigham. No more Brigham the intellectual snob, who could recite Chaucer by the ream and whose ambition was to teach a select class of sensitive students the delicate shades of Spenserian poetry.

Because he met a girl named Mary.

A quiet girl with a round pretty face, a shy smile, and a quick, wide-open mind.

Mary who poked fun at his classical mind, his snobbish plans. Mary who teased, prodded, argued. "Why don't you take Drake's course in American Education and Noyes' Nineteenth Century Thought. You might learn something."

Dr. Henry Noyes and Dr. W. E. Drake drew him out. Stirred him with subjects like "Are American Schools Free?"

"Mind in the Making." "Dare the Schools Build a New Order?"

A footnote in a textbook: Thousands of Missouri children were given no schooling because counties wouldn't set up separate schools for one or two Negro children, yet refused to accept them in the public schools.

"Mary, it's so stupidly unfair . . ."

"Well, why don't you find out more about it?"

Soon he was busy writing his doctorate on the History of Negro Education in Missouri.

When war came and the Army and Navy both turned him down because of bad eyesight, Missouri University offered him a job teaching freshman English at forty dollars a week. It was enough to get married on.

In one of his classes, a student wondered if she could write about the near-by state Negro university. "Why, of course. . . ."

When she read her paper in class, another student suggested that it might be a good idea to invite those Lincoln University students to a general forum, just to talk and learn about each other.

"Why of course . . ."

The forum went over so well, they held others. The students were enthusiastic. But one night Bob came home to Mary:

"I've just been told that if I don't stop holding these forums I'll find myself swinging from a tree with a rope around my neck."

"There's nothing wrong with what you're doing, Bob. You're not going to quit, are you?"

"God, if we can't practice simple democracy at a university, where can we practice it? If they want to lynch me, let them try. If they want to fire me—"

They fired him. One of the University's most highly respected English teachers wrote a letter to the college paper saying that Brigham was not being fired for incompetence but for "obnoxious associations." The letter was never printed. Students held protest meetings, signed petitions, made speeches. The University sat tight.

There were a dozen young teachers fired that semester. One elderly professor who helped them out, seriously offered some of them jobs writing greeting cards for a company he knew. Bob Brigham was made head of the English Department at Yankton.

When Bob and Mary felt they had done all they could at Yankton, they moved on to summer teaching at the University of Kansas City and Bob preached at Grandview. Now he's doing what Mary most wanted him to do—teaching teachers at Illinois State Normal University. But Mary isn't with him any more. She and her third child died of polio in childbirth. But Mary, who loved people and wanted them to think, to be decent, to fight the good fight, had helped to mold a man.

How many lives is a fort worth? A big, bell-shaped historic fort with fancy secret chambers and underground passages and even a ventilation system. What's it worth? Fifty casualties, a hundred, a thousand? How much is it worth? Do we have to take it now or can we take it later? How long shall we keep our troops there? Shall we do this or do that? Who wants to be a general?

32

DEATH OF A VETERAN

*T*he people kept crowding into the museum, filtering into Franklin D. Roosevelt's study, standing quietly behind the iron rail, staring at the things that used to be his: the shelves of books, the long desk, the pictures of old ships, the small-looking wheel chair in the corner.

A mother and her small son came in and the mother was explaining that this study belonged to President Roosevelt, who died last year. The little boy looked quickly around the room, his eyes lighting on the five small framed pictures of Fala.

"Is that his dog, Mama?"

His mother nodded.

"Did his dog die, too?"

They were mostly his neighbors, the people from Kingston and Poughkeepsie and the small towns across the river. The big city people were working and couldn't come. The others lived too far away.

Somebody estimated the crowd at five thousand but that wasn't right. There were millions there. The corporal sitting on a bench in the Champs Elysées, staring at the headline, repeating in a dull monotone, "I can't believe it. . . . I just can't believe it"; the tiny, living skeleton in Buchenwald who used to be a professor of languages in Czechoslovakia, saying, "I am not religious man but every morning I say God Bless President Roosevelt"; the scabby, skinny, barefoot Italian kid crying real tears and bawling, "Roosevelt Morte"; the old Negro watching the funeral train go by, rubbing the head of his small grandson, muttering, "I wish you were old enough to understand what you're seein'. You're seein' the funeral train of the greatest man who ever lived."

They were all there. . . .

"He called me Arthur," said Arthur Prettyman, who used to be Roosevelt's valet. "He was just about the most cheerful man you ever met in your life. I guess maybe he figured that there was no sense making everybody else feel bad, just because he had so many headaches."

Inside the high hedges, the photographers were lined up, impatiently waiting for President Truman and Mrs. Roosevelt to come and lay the wreath. From the way they talked, you could tell that for most of them, it was just another picture job. But if you searched the faces, you found the few who were deeply stirred. Like the short, thin photographer who kept staring at the grave for a long time, then snapped a picture, then stared some more and snapped another picture.

The photographer next to him poked him and kidded him about that. "Hey, Mac, what are you wasting film for? Nobody's around yet." The short thin man blushed a little, said nothing.

The pretty young woman was telling how the President had known her since she was eight years old, how she had ridden on his pony cart and swum with him in the swimming pool.

"And when it rained, all us kids would scoot up to that playroom up there," she said, pointing to a window on the second floor, "and he'd come around and make sure we all had some loganberry drink."

Her eyes grew warm. "I'll never forget that night on the porch when he called me over and said, 'Mag, come over and have your picture taken with your grandfather.' And the next day the picture was in all the papers. That was the night he had been nominated for president for the last time."

Even the kids who had noisily climbed up on the big trees on the lawn, even they were hushed when Mrs. Roosevelt started speaking.

"It was the people—all of the people of this country and of the world—whom my husband loved. He would want them to enjoy the rest and peace at Hyde Park just as he did all the days of his life."

She was still standing straight and tall when she finished, the sun shining flecks of light on her smiling face, and everybody who was seated, stood up to applaud.

Secretary of Interior Krug was the next speaker and the words he said were not pat words that come out smoothly. They were from deep inside, and you could hear his voice shake and see the paper tremble in his hands. Then President Truman, looking greyer and more tired than his pictures, saying, "We shall not soon see his like again." And when he said that, his lips tightened the same way they had tightened when he had stared at the grave.

After the speech, some of the bobby-soxers spotted Frank Sinatra at the edge of the porch and they let out with some wailing and screeching. One of the women said what a shame it was that these silly girls were upsetting the sacredness of the occasion. But somehow you felt that Franklin D. Roosevelt would have laughed at that.

The short man with the strange accent said that he had just arrived in this country, that he had never been here before.

"There couldn't be a more fitting beginning, could there?"

When the speakers had finished, the people lined up along the hedges to see his grave. There was no priority list of who stood first. It was simply a line of people who loved him, all kinds of people. Marion Anderson, an old couple each carrying a big basket of flowers, Leon Blum of France, Robert Sherwood, three solemn school kids, Mr. and Mrs. Herbert Lehman, a young girl drying her eyes—a long, long line.

The hats came off, the cigarettes were stepped on, the whispers were cut. And then, directly in front of the flower-covered grave, the momentary pause, the bowing of heads.

Stopping at the steps to the museum, the curator told the story of the time the building was first dedicated. There was a crowd of reporters and photographers, and Roosevelt stood on those steps and spoke without notes, telling how much all this meant to him, how many of his closest memories were inside that building.

"Then right after he finished," said the curator, "there was a second's silence and then this newsreel photographer blurted out that he'd like Mr. Roosevelt to repeat the speech because he hadn't caught all of it. And Roosevelt just looked at the man and you could see the hurt expression on his face when he said, 'Don't you understand. . . . that's something you can't repeat. . . .'"

Most of the people were wandering around, staring at the Arabian jewels, the tapestries sent from the Dalai Lama of Tibet, the Kiksadi totem pole, the golf trophies he won at Campobello in 1895, and the largest ice boat ever built that belonged to his uncle.

But it was quiet inside his library. There were all kinds of books from *Alice's Adventures in Wonderland*, first Italian edition, 1872, to *An Epistle containing the Strange Medical Experiences of Karsish, the Arab Browning* (in Braille).